The Man In The Dugout

THE STORY OF JULIAN MOCK

Randy Blalock

Copyright © 2016 Randy Blalock
All rights reserved.

ISBN: 1530363608
ISBN 13: 9781530363605

*DEDICATED TO MISS DOT,
TERRY, ALAN, AND CHRISTY.
THANK YOU FOR SHARING
YOUR HUSBAND AND YOUR FATHER
WITH ALL OF US.*

Foreword

In the journey known as life, there are certain people that you meet who possess life qualities and leadership skills that separate them from most. If you're fortunate enough to befriend these individuals, it can be life changing. This was the case for me when my life's path crossed that of Julian Mock.

Julian is a true southern gentleman- small in stature, but large in heart and compassion. He is a quick-witted, eloquently-stated gentleman who carries himself with class and character at all times. Never short on having fun or knowing the proper thing to say or how to put people at ease. Julian has a presence.

The professor, as he is known by his baseball friends, takes great pride in sharing and training young baseball personnel. Julian has a gift in telling stories and sharing lessons. His audiences would hang on his every word. It was his gift to "hand down" generational practices and wisdom of baseball in all aspects of our great game. His ability to preach the gospel of baseball in a way that would affect you both short term and long term touched so many of us that are still working in the game today. His lessons also carried over to the game of life. He would discuss his priorities of life: God, family, then job. This was never ego-driven, as Julian would always place others above himself.

Julian was always willing to help open doors that would allow players places to play, recommend players to coaches for their programs, and provide references for some of us to get into professional baseball. People trusted Julian because they knew of his credibility and character.

It is my wish that you will emerge yourself in this book about Julian Mock, a true professional in every sense of the word. A tremendous talent evaluator, it was once said, "bring the players into the stadium and the little man will tell em who can play." Enjoy the journey of a true difference-maker whose values and abilities helped so many of us who are blessed to call him our friend.

Here's hoping that your life's journey will allow you to meet someone who will believe in you and provide a blueprint to follow as Julian Mock has done for me and for so many others who've had the good fortune to cross his path. Happy reading!

Dan Jennings
Special Assistant to the General Manager
Washington Nationals Baseball Club

Warmup

For three consecutive days during the late spring of 1961, rain had fallen causing the delay of the third and deciding game of what had been an epic City Championship baseball series between the Sylvan Hills Golden Bears and the Murphy War Eagles. Regardless of the level of play, high school, college, or professional, few series could equal the quality of play seen during this competition.

Murphy, from the eastern division, had not lost a game going into the best two of three series and Sylvan, playing in the western division for the City of Atlanta, had but one loss themselves. There was no question that these were the two best teams coming out of Atlanta. In fact, it was the second year in a row that they were meeting for the city championship. Murphy, on its way to becoming State Champ, had bested the Bears in 1960 to take the city crown. And here they were, facing each other again.

Not only was the City Championship on the line, a trip to the State Finals hung in the balance. Only the winner could advance. It was evident that there was considerable pressure on the players from both teams. The pressure did not seem to affect the pitching, however.

The first game of the series was to be played at the home field of Sylvan. Their ace, left hander Tommy Chapman, was to face Murphy right hander, Weldon Crook. Chapman was, literally, unhittable that day and Sylvan coasted to an easy victory on the strength of his no-hitter.

Facing elimination, Murphy came home to its home field on Clifton Street in southeast Atlanta. Not to be outdone by Sylvan's Chapman, Murphy's ace, right hander David Guthrie, tossed his own no-hitter as Murphy defeated Sylvan setting up the third and decisive game. Two games- two no-hitters. Then the rains came.

Danny Tate, shortstop for Murphy and member of the previous year's State Championship team, remembers pacing around his house for three days anxious to play the game. "We'd go to the gym to toss the ball around but we couldn't take BP (batting practice) or infield practice so, there was a lot of nervous energy being used up. The only good thing about our predicament was that we knew Sylvan was going through the same thing."

Finally, the skies cleared enough for the game to be played. The final game was to be played at a neutral field but there seems to be a discrepancy of those involved in the game as to exactly where the game was held. Some say it was Georgia Tech's Rose Bowl Field (now Russ Chandler Stadium). The field, located near Fifth and Fowler Streets inside the campus of Georgia Tech, derived its name because it had been built in 1930 from the proceeds Georgia Tech earned from playing in the Rose Bowl football game the previous year. But others, and most importantly, the coach involved in the game that day, say it was at Atlantic Steel Company so we will go with that. The location of the game is not as important as what happened that day. Because the rains had persisted for three days, both aces, Chapman and Guthrie, would have had enough rest to allow them to pitch again.

As if the first two games had not been dramatic enough, the third game proved to be just as exciting. Both pitchers were, once again, magnificent. Chapman had only given up one meaningless hit in the first five innings but Guthrie had faced the first fifteen batters without allowing a single base runner. The defense had played flawlessly behind him although they had not had many opportunities since Guthrie had struck out nine of the fifteen batters he had faced. Guthrie had been perfect through five.

Fifty plus years have passed since this game so the memories of those who participated in the game have, in their words, become fuzzy. The runner and batter change from telling to telling but the strategy used by the man standing in the third base coach's box does not. Let's just say it happened this way.

Jimmy "Yardbird" Battle, Murphy's second baseman, leads off the top of the sixth with a solid single over the head of Sylvan's second baseman. Jere Ard is the next batter. The batter is given his sign and being a team built on solid fundamentals, he lays down a perfect bunt sending Battle to second. One out.

The next batter is Murphy's left fielder, Mike Fisher. The outfield of Sylvan is playing in to cut down the runner, Battle, now standing on second. Fisher connects with a solid single but Sylvan's left fielder fields the ball perfectly and throws a strike to home plate. The coach in the third base box sees that the fielder has made a good play but he also sees that Battle, because of the wet base paths caused by the rain, has slipped slightly. He holds Battle at third. But seeing that the ball was thrown to home, Fisher keeps running, as he has been taught, but is thrown out at second with a perfect throw from the catcher. Runner on third- two out.

That brings up Roy Jarrett. Jarrett was a three sport letterman and probably the best all-around athlete Murphy ever produced. He would go on to play both football and baseball for Georgia Tech. The coach eyes the pitcher with intensity looking for any edge he might be able to find. The pitch is delivered and it hits the outside corner for strike one. The coach asks for time out from the umpire and calls Jarrett to him. He places his arm around the young boy seemingly giving him encouragement as well as instructions. The bleachers on both the first base side and third base side are filled with screaming fans for the two teams. The on deck batter yells to Jarrett, "C'mon, Roy! You can do it!"

Jarrett stares at the pitcher as he takes the mound for the next pitch daring him to throw another strike. Always the keen observer, the coach has noticed a small flaw in the pitcher's delivery. Right before he delivers his pitch to the plate, he dips his head taking his eyes off the batter. The pitcher begins his wind up and in the middle of his arm swing, just as he averts his eyes, Jarrett calmly steps out of the batter's box. The pitcher, now looking up to see no batter in the box and obviously confused, stops his motion. There is a deafening hush from the crowd that is broken only by the umpire's call- "Balk!" waving Battle in from third. The Murphy dugout erupts as the first run of the game is scored.

But there is still work to be done. Guthrie retires the side in the sixth and Murphy still leads 1-0 as he takes the mound trying to get the last three outs. Wayne McDaniel was the catcher that day and he recalls being terrified as he took his place behind home plate. "Guthrie could really throw hard and I was scared to death that I would allow a passed ball or do something else stupid that would mess up his perfect game."

The man we called Coach stood in the dugout giving directions to his players in the field as they prepared for the seventh and, hopefully, final inning. Knowing that as well as Guthrie was pitching, it would be highly unlikely that a Sylvan player could pull the ball on him, he motioned for the shortstop and left fielder to move to their lefts, protecting the middle of the field more. Yet, just in case the right-handed batter got lucky, he had the third baseman, Larry Greene, protect the line to guard against an extra base hit down the line.

Guthrie got the first two outs easily but ran the count to 3-2 on Sylvan's last hope. McDaniel said that David then threw the fastest pitch he had all afternoon and the batter just froze, taking it for a called third strike. The dugout erupted once again. Fans raced onto the field. Bedlam ensued as Murphy celebrated their second consecutive City Championship.

Calmly looking on with a huge grin on his face was Coach Julian Mock- the man who had seen that the Sylvan pitcher was working from a full windup, not the stretch, making him more susceptible to balking. The man who had his team so fundamentally sound that they could take advantage of the smallest opportunity and turn it into victory. A coach so far ahead of his time and whose baseball savvy was so pronounced that his former players, without exception, revere him to this very day. This is his story.

But it is also a story of a man who was much more than just a high school baseball coach. This is a story of a young boy growing up in a small town in Alabama. This is a story of a young boy who loved the game of baseball and, while not the most gifted player ever to wear spikes, found a way to make his high school team and later to play for Auburn. This is the story of a young man who served his country in the military and while serving, met the love of his life. This is the story of a man who became one of the most respected baseball scouts in the country.

But it is also the story of a son, a brother, a husband, a father, a grand-dad, a respected educator, and a mentor to those of us lucky enough to call him Coach. This is the story of-----

THE MAN IN THE DUGOUT

1st Inning

"Growing Up In Alabama"

Peter Robert Mock walked into the small general store located in the middle of the town of Selma, Alabama that late-May morning in 1929 to pick up a few things his wife had requested. Before he left, he had made sure that his wife, Lanora, could handle their two boys, Peter Robert, Jr., or PR as he was known who was three, and James Webb Mock, age two, by herself in his absence. She just laughed at him and told him, "What do you think I've been doing these last nine months while you go off to work every day? Now, off with ya' but get back quick cause I need that washing detergent to take care of these boys' dirty clothes."

The Mocks were expecting their third child and the birth could happen any time so Peter wanted to make sure she was comfortable before he made the trip. He told her, "Well, they're still asleep right now so you just sit down with your cup of coffee and relax as best you can."

Upon entering the store, he was greeted by several other men who were involved in a game of checkers.

"How's everything going, Mock?" one of the men shouted. No further explanation was needed of the question since everyone in town knew of the pending arrival.

"Heard you're hopin' for a girl this time." another said.

Peter Mock let a small grin cross his face which gave away his feelings. "Lanora's doing fine. Just ready to have the baby before it gets much hotter. And, yeah, after them two boys she's all set to have a little girl around the house. But, you know, we don't really care as long as it is healthy. Doc says it cain't be much longer so I got another fella doing my route for me today."

Peter Mock hurriedly continued with his shopping so that he could get back to the house. The last thing he wanted was to get involved in a long conversation with these guys. He didn't have time to talk about the latest Laurel and Hardy movie- their first talkie that had just hit the movie houses in Montgomery. And even though he was a huge baseball fan, he couldn't get caught up with talking about the no-hitter the great Carl Hubbell had thrown against the Pirates earlier that month. Those discussions would have to wait for another day.

Peter Mock was lucky to have a job. So many in this part of Alabama and, for that matter, the rest of the country didn't. Economic conditions were getting worse all the time but his income kept a roof over their heads and clothes on their backs. Most of their food came from trading with others who farmed like he did. While he raised mostly corn and cotton on their seventy acres, he was able to swap out for other food items from various neighbors.

But farming was not his primary income source. He had taken the Civil Service exam awhile back and now worked for the Post Office. In the mornings he would sort the mail and wait on walk-up customers but then he would begin his route as a rural carrier. Delivering the mail over such a wide area would usually take him to late afternoon, when he would come home and head straight to the fields. Along with his hired hand, Otis, the two of them would do whatever was necessary, depending on the time of year, until it got dark.

The dawn broke on the morning of Tuesday, May 21, 1929 to cries of pain coming from Lanora. It was time for the baby. Peter gathered her things, helped her to the car, and shuffled the boys in the back seat. He dropped them off at the nearest neighbor's house where they would be tended to while Lanora was in the hospital. Peter apologized to the neighbor as he raced the boys to her door, "James has been awful colicky the last couple of days. A little Vaseline seems to do the trick."

Travelling the mostly unpaved roads was difficult for Lanora, whose contractions had gotten pretty regular, but they arrived at Selma Hospital, the same hospital where she would later work herself, in plenty of time. Both Peter, from Mt. Vernon, Alabama, and Lanora, from even smaller Butler, Alabama were used to everyone knowing your business but they were also accustomed to special small-town treatment from those they knew. Lanora was whisked into the hospital as soon as the nurses saw who she was.

Peter filled out all the paperwork while Sally and Allie took her upstairs to the maternity ward. Peter walked up to the second floor and went straight to the waiting room. No one else was there, so he took time to say a little prayer. Peter was not a church-goer like Lanora, but he still knew who was in charge at this moment.

A nurse came out about two hours later with an update that his wife was progressing but that there was still going to be a little wait before the baby arrived. He had not slept well the night before- hadn't slept well in over a week actually, nervous about the arrival. Each twist and turn that Lanora made in bed, each little sigh or audible groan she made put him on high alert that something was about to happen. He didn't remember being so nervous when PR or James came into the world but the hopeful anticipation of having a girl made this pregnancy different.

An elderly neighbor lady arrived to sit with him. Miss Elsie was known to "talk your ears off", but she was noticeably quiet today, much to Peter's relief.

Finally, the doors opened from the delivery room and Peter heard the beautiful sound of a wailing baby. The doctor was smiling as he approached Peter. "Everybody's fine- Lanora and the baby." Knowing that Peter was a big baseball fan, he said, "Peter, it looks like you're on your way to a ball team of your own. Congratulations! It's a boy!"

Miss Elsie jumped up and gave Peter a hug and a big smack on his cheek. She asked, "What cha' gonna name him?"

With a bewildered look he replied, "I have no idea. We were so sure this one was gonna be a girl, that we didn't give no boys name a second thought."

The doctor smiled at him and said, "Well, don't be worrying about that just yet. You've got time to think about it. We don't need to fill out that birth certificate until ya'll leave and that won't be for a few days yet."

The exhaustion and stress of the last few days finally got to Peter and he slumped down into the nearest chair. Miss Elsie said, "You go see about Lanora and I'll go make sure there's plenty of food for ya'll when you get home."

Peter nodded his approval, which also served as his unspoken thanks to Miss Elsie and asked the Doc when he could see Lanora.

"It'll take her a little while to wake up but you can go see the boy as soon as they clean him up." The two men shook hands and the doctor turned back down the hall to check on a lady who had delivered twins the day before.

Peter walked down to the window and looked in on the two baby girls wriggling around in their pink blankets. His new baby was not there yet but as soon as the nurse entered carrying his new little boy, his heart filled with joy. He thought to himself, a little brother will be good for the two older boys. It'll teach them some responsibility in taking care of a younger brother. Course, they'll probably be more fights I'll have to break up, too.

After the nurse laid him in his crib, Peter just stared at the new infant. He was making an awful lot of racket and throwing his arms and legs around like a little bucking bronco. He thought to himself- "Buck, that'll be his nickname." Another nurse tapped him on his shoulder breaking him out of his reverie and told him he could go see Lanora now.

A third nurse was brushing Lanora's hair as he entered her room. Since there was only the one other birth, she had the room to herself. Peter walked over to her and kissed her forehead. "That's all I get?" she asked. He looked at the other woman in the room and shyly bent down further to give her a kiss.

"We need to give the baby a name." Peter said.

Lanora replied, "Well, even though we were hopin' for a girl, I've been givin' it some thought. I'd like his middle name to be my maiden name- Rogers. And I want to call him Julian."

"Julian!" Peter snapped. "Why, that's a girl's name!"

"No, it ain't! It's actually French and that's where your people are originally from and there was once a Roman Emperor named Julian. I been studying it. And the best part to me is that Julian means "youthful" and he'll be the youngest so it makes sense."

Peter knew that once she made her mind up, nothing he could say or do would unchange it, so, he nodded and said, "If that's what you want, honey, that's what it'll be." But to himself he thought, "I hope he can fight cause he's gonna take a lot of kidding about that name."

Julian Rogers Mock was born on May 21, 1929.

Christmas was going to be very special for the Mock boys, PR, James, and Julian in the year 1937. They had been poring over the Sears catalog for months leading up to the big day and had let it be known in no uncertain terms what was on their list- baseball equipment.

Peter had put some money aside each week so that the boys could have their first special Christmas in quite a few years. The country was finally coming out of the Depression and even though Peter had been steadily employed by the Post Office, things had been really tight in the early Thirties.

In early December of that year he had taken the boys out to find their tree. Even though most of their land was used for farm land, several acres were wooded and they could always find a good tree to use as their Christmas tree. Decorating the tree was a special treat because it meant there would be plenty of popcorn and sugar cookies left over after they were used as the homemade decorations that went on the tree. There was one very special ornament, however, that went on the top of the tree. Lanora had kept a beautiful crocheted angel from her childhood that always adorned the top. As the youngest, it was Julian's job to place it on the top. Peter would lift him up and Julian would proudly announce, "And that is the angel who came to Mary telling her she was going to have Baby Jesus."

The boys had been brought up attending church each Sunday, Lanora made sure of that, so, they were very familiar with the Christmas story.

James had even won an award the year before for reciting the Nativity Story from Luke 2 by heart.

Like all siblings, the three boys fought and argued. James once threw a brick at PR and PR, being the oldest and biggest, was continuously pushing Julian down. But even though he was the smallest, Julian's feisty spirit didn't allow the bullying so, he would jump up and flail punches at anyone who tried to take advantage of him. He didn't win any of the fights but he let it be known that he was not intimidated.

Christmas morning finally arrived and when they charged out of their bedroom they saw the usual array of gifts that Santa brought; underwear, socks, a bag of fruit, and a toy or two but none of them saw what they were really looking for. Peter and Lanora just stood back with little smiles on their faces. The boys showed respectful appreciation, but there was no doubt they were disappointed.

Not a word was said during breakfast about what wasn't under the tree- the boys knew better than that and Peter and Lanora went along with the joke a little longer. Finally, they couldn't hold back anymore. They told the boys to sit down, that Santa had left each of them one more present but they couldn't have it until after breakfast. Lanora went into the room and brought out three beautifully wrapped presents handing one to PR, one to James, and one to Julian.

Peter said to them, "Before you open them, Santa said that you have to share them. Can you boys do that without getting into fights?" Three heads vigorously nodded up and down. "Okay- open them up."

With squeals of delight, they tore into the paper. James finished first and because of its shape, he knew what it was. "A real Hillerich & Bradsby baseball bat!" he exclaimed. "No more using big sticks as bats!"

PR opened his box to find an official Spalding baseball. The ball was so shiny and white that it almost glowed. PR caressed the stitches, imagining that he was Dizzy Dean, his favorite player from the St. Louis Cardinals, throwing a curve ball to strike out New York Giants slugger Mel Ott in the bottom of the ninth.

Julian was rendered speechless as he opened his box to find a brand new fielder's glove. But what made it extra special was that it was an autographed Joe DiMaggio glove. Julian had idolized DiMaggio from the first time he could read the sports pages from the newspapers.

Even though it was below freezing the boys begged their mom to let them go outside and play with their new gear. There was no way she could say no. After making sure they were bundled up properly, the boys ran outside. They would take turns as one would pitch to another while the third fielded. Peter watched from the window and said to Lanora, "You know, Julian is already better than his bothers. He catches everything hit his way and for his size, he can smack the daylights out of the ball. Come watch him, Lanora. He can almost hit it all the way to the road."

Julian, while he threw right handed, batted left handed and, sure enough on the next pitch from James, smacked a solid line drive that PR had no chance of catching as it sailed over his head. Even James was impressed saying, "You smacked the snot out of that one!"

After the Christmas break, the boys got back into their daily routines which included rising before daybreak to feed the poultry and pigs, milk the cow, and muck the stable. The boys took turns with these chores and the biggest fights they ever had was in determining whose turn it was to shovel the manure.

After a hearty breakfast, they would gather their books and head off to school. Their walk was not too far since the one-room schoolhouse, which went by the name of Oak Grove School, was actually located on their property. Peter leased the building to the local school board. The school consisted of one teacher and 10-15 students ranging from the first to fifth grades. The teacher taught all subjects. She would break them into their respective age groups during the day for particular levels of learning such as math and science but that had its drawbacks since she was not able to devote her entire day to that group. Therefore, a lot of things got left out. Julian would later say that he did not really learn how to read properly during these years. He had to develop his reading skills on his own.

After school the boys hurried to the fields where they were expected to help their dad and Otis with the work that needed to be done there. Mr. Mock usually let them go home before sunset so they could get a little play time in before supper and doing their homework. Then, it was off to bed so that they could start the same routine the next day.

All that hard work made Saturdays very special. Peter, Lanora and the three boys would pile into the family car and head to town. While their Mom would go shopping for groceries and other family necessities, Dad would pick up farming supplies. The boys were each given a dime so they could go to the local movie theater to see, as Julian called them, the current "shoot-em-ups". These were the suspenseful serials that would leave you hanging at the end of each episode wondering what was going to happen to the hero. Did he survive the fall from the cliff? Did the damsel in distress get rescued? You had to go back the following week to find out.

And what boy didn't like the cartoons? Mickey Mouse, Daffy Duck, and the Disney feature *Ferdinand the Bull* were all popular, but Julian's favorite was Popeye. And the main feature, usually a western or a pirate movie, made the day special indeed. That is, unless you got in trouble.

The boys had worked extra hard one week so Peter gave each of them an additional nickel so they could each buy a bag of popcorn. They sat near the back of the theater munching their snack and enjoying Errol Flynn in *The Adventures of Robin Hood*. It was a boring part of the picture when Robin and Maid Marian were all "lovey dovey" so, PR turns to James and makes a motion as if he was busting the now empty bag of popcorn. The message got down to Julian and in quick succession, PR, then James, then Julian busted their bags making loud pops that were heard throughout the theater startling several patrons around them.

The boys were rolling in their seats with laughter but it only took a few seconds for Mrs. Carter, the ticket lady, to roar into the theater, yank the boys out of their seats, and escort them down to the general store where she knew Peter would be. As stern Mrs. Carter approached with the boys close in tow, he listened intently to her demand that they be punished for their misdeed. Peter nodded and assured her that he would definitely tan their backsides. The boys were terrified because he was a belt-whipper and they feared the worse.

After Mrs. Carter was out of sight, he looked at them sternly and asked them, "Do you know what you did was wrong?" Three heads bobbed up and down in unison. "Do you promise not to do that again?" Three contrite nods were the responses. "Then we'll just forget this happened." He then smiled at them and admitted, "How can I get mad at you when I did the same thing when I was your age except I did it in church." The four of them laughed. Then he added, "But tell your Mom I paddled your butts if she asks."

The weekend was completed on Sundays with church attendance. Julian cannot remember missing many Sundays and he took pride in his early Christian training. The family, with the exception of Dad who stayed home so that, in Lanora's words, he could attend to things, would drive up to the local Baptist church.

Julian admits to having a little bit of a temper and it came out in full force one particular Sunday. Many of us who attended Baptist churches can remember fondly the offering envelope you turned in each week. Not only did you put in your offering, but on the outside of the envelope were boxes you were supposed to check indicating how faithful you had been to your other Christian duties. You checked if you brought your Bible to Sunday School. You checked if you had read your daily Bible verses. And you checked if you attended the Worship Service.

For some reason, and Julian does not recall exactly why, they never attended the church service. He thinks it was because their Dad needed the car but is not positive on that account. In any event, Julian could never check that box, so he could never claim 100% on his envelope.

One Sunday, a bigger boy in the class accosted him on this point claiming that Julian was bringing their class down by never being 100%. Julian took exception to this remark. Truth is, he took a lot of exception- so much exception that he bounced out of his chair and punched the boy right in the mouth. Julian could not escape the belt on this one and remembers that it was the worst whipping he ever got.

But church attendance did have its benefits in ways beyond the obvious. Attending Sunday School each week gave Julian the chance to meet a man that he calls one of the biggest positive influences in his life- his Sunday School teacher, Jere Hardy.

Mr. Hardy was one of those people who could be stern and strict inside the classroom, but friendly and helpful outside of it. Hardy made sure that the boys listened attentively to his lessons but was often seen playing pitch with them or tossing a football around the church grounds afterwards. And for some reason, Julian remembers, he took a special interest in him. Because of Jere Hardy, Julian was going to attend his first baseball game.

Julian's love for baseball grew with the years. He played other sports with his brothers and other guys, but being relatively small for his age, he couldn't compete as well in football and basketball as he could in baseball where his skills continued to be superior to most of the other boys. Julian absorbed everything he could about the game. Working at the Post Office, his Dad was able to bring a newspaper home each day and as soon as Peter arrived, Julian would tear into the sports section.

The first thing he would check would be the New York Yankees box score to see what his hero, Joe DiMaggio, had done the previous day. If the "Yankee Clipper" had gone 3x4, he would smile broadly, but on those rare occasions when Joe might go 0x4, Julian would pout and stomp outside to let off some steam.

One day in the early spring of 1938, he opened the paper and discovered an announcement that made him burst with excitement. The Cincinnati Redlegs were coming to Selma to play an exhibition game before they headed north to begin their season. Julian jumped up and with the glee only nine year-olds can possess, ran to find his Dad asking, "Can we go? Can we go?"

Cincinnati was one of the better teams in the National League at that time. They featured several players who were household names to baseball fans across the country- players who would make baseball history and one that would make the Hall of Fame.

Ernie Lombardi was an eight-time All-Star and one of the best hitting catchers ever. He would actually go on to win the Most Valuable Player Award in 1938 leading the Redlegs to their best finish (fourth place) in over a decade. In 1939, however, they won the National League pennant but were swept in the World Series by the powerful New York Yankees. It was during this series that Lombardi was involved in one of the most famous plays in World Series history.

Lombardi, known as "The Schnoz" for his rather bulbous nose, was taking a throw from the outfield trying to tag a charging Yankee runner out at the plate. The runner slid and inadvertently spiked Lombardi in the groin. Lombardi was not wearing a protective cup that day. In considerable pain, Lombardi laid spread eagle on the ground with his massive body lying on the ball preventing any of his teammates from retrieving it. This allowed the player who had hit the ball, ironically Joe DiMaggio, to come all the way around the bases to score. The play is referred to as "Lombardi's Big Snooze" because it looked like he was asleep while lying on his back.

Another interesting note about Lombardi was that he was, perhaps, the slowest man ever to play the game making his hitting statistics more impressive because, as one teammate said, "He'd have to hit the ball to the wall just to get a single." And his manager once told a reporter, "We time the other players going from first to third with a stop watch. We time Lombardi with a sun dial."

Another prominent member of that team and a player who would make baseball history during the 1938 season was pitcher, Johnny Vander Meer. Vander Meer is the only pitcher in Major League history to throw back-to-back no-hitters.

1938 would be Vander Meer's second season in the majors after an unimpressive first season. But on June 11, 1938, he threw his first no-hitter against the Boston Braves. Four days later against the Brooklyn Dodgers in what would be the first night game ever played at Ebbets

Field, he threw another no-hitter. Vander Meer would be named the starting pitcher for the National League in the All-Star game that year and lead them to their first win over the American League in the last five years. Vander Meer was never able to have another season like 1938, however, and finished his career with a losing record.

Julian's Dad looked at him with sadness telling him, "Buck, I just don't see how. It wouldn't be fair for just you to go- PR and James will certainly want to go, too, and we just don't have enough extra money for all of us to go. If you want to go, you'll just have to find another way." Julian didn't cry- but he felt like it.

That night after supper as Julian helped his mother with the dishes, it was his turn to dry, Lanora sensed that something was wrong. Julian had been unusually quiet during the meal even when the two older boys teased him about having a girlfriend at school. As they stood there at the sink together with no one else around, she asked him what was troubling him. Julian shared his disappointment about not being able to attend the game. "Mom, it would be the first time I ever got to see a real game and I was just hoping we could go."

Like any mother, her heart sank as she looked into his eyes. She knew of only one person who might help make his dream come true. The next Sunday she sought out Jere Hardy for advice. He told her that he would ask some of his friends if they would be willing to sponsor Julian or, perhaps, pay him in advance for work they needed done. But after a momentary hesitation he added that there might be another way. "Does Julian belong to the Knot Hole Gang? I understand that boys who are members get free admission to the games. Maybe that includes this game, too. And I'll be glad to nominate him. My signature and yours will get him in the club."

The first Knot Hole Gang was established by the St. Louis Cardinal organization at the height of the Depression. A St. Louis businessman wanted to recognize the exemplary youth of his city by donating tickets to each Cardinal game to deserving boys of the community. These boys had to be nominated by citizens and then, after completing a form that was signed by them and a parent, the boy was a member. The name of the organization came from the days when most ballparks were made of wood. Young boys would find knotholes in the outfield fence, poke them out, and watch the game through the hole; hence Knot Hole Gang.

Mr. Hardy filled out the form and gave it to Julian one Sunday telling him its purpose. Julian was so happy that he did something he rarely did- he gave Mr. Hardy a big hug.

The day of the game finally arrived and Julian's excitement was overflowing. It was all he could do to keep from boasting to his brothers that he was going to the game and they weren't. But he knew that if he did, (a) his Dad would not allow him to go and (b) they would beat him senseless so he wisely kept his mouth shut.

As soon as Sunday School was over, he raced to the car and waited impatiently as his Mother seemed to talk to every other member of the Baptist Church. He even considered blowing the horn to speed her up but knew that would not be a smart thing to do either. They finally made it home where he changed out of his church clothes into his dungarees, t-shirt, and baseball cap. He grabbed his glove in case any foul balls came his way and he and his mom set out for the ballpark.

Upon arriving at the field, Lanora parked the car so she could go up to the ticket booth with him. Julian had remembered to bring his membership certificate and he placed it proudly in the window anxiously waiting for his ticket.

"Not good today!" the man in the booth said, hardly looking up from his newspaper.

"What do you mean not good today? It's been filled out properly and signed by two people, just like it's supposed to be- what do you mean not good today?" Julian's Mom asked.

"I mean it is not good today." the man responded surly. "Today is Sunday and Knot Hole tickets are not accepted on Sundays."

There are few things that tear at a young boys heart more than broken dreams and that was certainly the case for young Julian. Despite the earnest efforts of a loving mother and a respected mentor, this dream, the dream of seeing a real game with actual professional players, was not happening today. Even his brothers, jealous at first of his good fortune, knew that they shouldn't tease him. For Julian it was a very long and disappointing day.

Julian finished at the elementary school in 1940 and attended Dallas Academy for his sixth grade year. On promotion to the seventh grade, Julian attended Selma Junior High through the eighth grade. While in Junior High, he played both basketball and baseball. It was during his seventh grade year that one of the most significant dates in American History took place.

It was early December, 1941, and the boys now 15, 14, and 12 were looking forward to the upcoming holiday vacation from school. One Sunday morning, the entire family was sitting in the living room listening to the radio, the only means of home entertainment the family had. A fire was roaring in the fireplace and the boys were arguing over whose turn it was to go outside into the cold to retrieve more firewood. By a vote of 2-1, it was determined that James would have to battle the freezing temperatures outside. Suddenly, a news bulletin interrupted the Jack Benny Show they were listening to.

"We have just received this information from the Armed Services Radio Network. Pearl Harbor; Honolulu, Hawaii. A large contingent of Japanese aircraft have attacked the naval base at Pearl Harbor early this morning. Early reports indicate significant damage to numerous ships anchored at the base along with damage to aircraft. There are reports of extensive casualties and injuries to the servicemen and women stationed there but no numbers have been released as yet. This was a totally unwarranted and ruthless attack by a nation that we were, supposedly, at peace with. In fact, a group of Japanese delegates had just met with American officials to outline a plan for peaceful coexistence. This was obviously a ruse set up by a group of diabolical leaders of a war-seeking government."

All five Mocks sat there in stunned silence. The threat of war had hung over the country ever since Germany, under the demented leadership of Adolph Hitler, had invaded Poland in 1939. But the American public thought the war would be fought in Europe, not in the Pacific Ocean.

The next day the United States declared war on Japan and Franklin Delano Roosevelt's famous words that the "day will live in infamy" rang true. Even though the two older boys were ready to enlist the next day out of youthful exuberance, their ages would prevent them from doing so for a few more years.

Even in times of war, the mail must go through so, Peter had job security during the war years since most of the younger men in Selma were fighting overseas. Now that the boys could pretty much take care of themselves, Lanora picked up extra money for the household by tending to the children of young mothers who had to have jobs to support the family while their husbands were in the service.

Sports continued to play a large part in Julian's life. And when he was not playing baseball during the summers, he could usually be found near water either fishing or swimming, his two other favorite pastimes. One of his favorite memories from those years, but one that had somewhat dangerous overtones, took place in 1943, the summer between his 8th and 9th grade year. He was looking forward to entering Parrish High School where he would join his two older brothers. But he was also hopeful that he would be good enough to play for one of the best coaches in all of Alabama- Comer Sims.

But first, he planned to enjoy that summer. Julian had just turned 14 and even though their Dad kept them busy helping with the farm work, there was still some leisure time available. The boys had put their heads together and come up with a plan to swim across the nearby Alabama River. None of them had ever attempted this before and even though the distance was not that great (the river was usually no more than about ¾ mile across) the fairly strong currents made the crossing treacherous. All three were good swimmers but even the best of swimmers would have problems in those rough waters. But what do three daring teenagers know about caution?

The Alabama River is formed by the merging of the Tallapoosa and Coosa Rivers just six miles north of Montgomery, Alabama. It is a meandering river that travels a total of 318 miles. After passing through Montgomery, the river flows west to Selma where it then turns in a southwesterly direction and continues to Mobile. Because the elevation of the surrounding terrain is always decreasing, the river has spots where it travels at speeds causing rapids and rough water. This was the type of dangerous waters the boys were planning to cross that day.

Lanora was babysitting that morning and Peter was at the post office so the boys prepared a few sandwiches for themselves along with some cookies. That would be their lunch before they began their swim. They had discussed their plans in the sanctity of their bedroom several times. The plan was simple. They would hike down to the river entry spot they had scouted out- a walk of about three miles from their house. They'd eat their lunch and after a sufficient wait to let their food digest, they'd begin their swimming adventure. After reaching the other bank, they'd walk down to the newly-constructed Edmund Pettis Bridge, cross over into Selma and walk back home.

If the name of the bridge sounds familiar, it should. This bridge would later have historical significance as the site of the famous Selma Civil Rights March on March 7, 1965. This particular bridge was selected by the leaders of the movement, most notably Martin Luther King, Jr. and Andrew Young, in defiance of its namesake. Edmund Pettis had been a Civil War General as well as a US Senator representing Alabama. But he had also been the Alabama Grand Dragon of the KKK.

The boys had chosen a day that turned out to be overcast and even muggier than typical mid-Alabama weather in July. By the time they reached their diving in point, they were already dripping with sweat and tired from the walk. They sat down to enjoy their meal and to finalize their plans.

PR opened the discussion by asking, "Are you two sure you want to do this?"

Always ready for any type of challenge, Julian piped in quickly, "You bet. There'll be nothing to it. We're good swimmers. What could go wrong?"

James, or Buddy as he was called by the family just like Julian was always Buck, was not as confidant. "That river looks like its flowing pretty strong. All that rain we've had over the past few days has swelled the banks. Maybe we need to wait until its gone down a little."

"Come on, ya big chickin'. It's not that far across. We can make it easy." PR chided. "I've got an idea. We'll take our clothes off and skinny dip across. That'll make us lighter and the clothes won't weigh us down."

The other two boys agreed that that sounded like a good idea. Of course, they hadn't thought about how they would retrieve their clothes once on the other side. There was nothing left to do now but to do it. They stripped down to their skivvies and inched closer to the bank. None of them were willing to be the first in until little Julian let out a war whoop and dove into the river. The other two followed closely afterward.

Because of the age difference, PR and James soon caught up with and passed Julian but all three recognized the challenge that the river presented immediately. The river was flowing from their right to left and it seemed that for every stroke they took forward, they would have to take two to get back on course. What would have been a challenging distance in calm waters turned into a major physical exercise.

As they got to within 200 yards from the bank, James began to tire out and started floundering in the water. He began thrashing about, using more energy, rather than taking smooth strokes. PR saw that he was struggling so he floated back to assist him. Julian, too, was tiring quickly but he pressed on. With grit and determination not to give in, he continued to pump his arms until he could pump no longer. But it was at that moment that he felt the bottom of the river bed. He literally crawled the last few yards until he made it to the bank, pulling himself into the grass and collapsing. He looked back to see PR and James stagger out of the water, crawl up the bank and fall down panting for breath next to him. It was several minutes before anyone could talk.

Always competitive, especially against his older brothers, Julian said, "I won. I got here first." PR and James replied, "Jerk!"

Soaking wet, but now that the challenge had been won, filled with exhilaration, the boys looked down, realized that they had no clothes and wondered how they would make it back home. "We can't walk through town naked." James said.

"No, you can't!" came a voice from the woods behind them. Out from the underbrush stepped their Dad.

Almost in unison, all three boys asked, "Dad, what're you doing here?"

"Well," he admitted, "I overheard your plans and thought it might be a good idea for me to keep a watch out for you in case you got in trouble and for a moment I thought I was going to have to jump in. James, are you okay?" James gave an embarrassed nod that he was.

"I was hiding in the bushes over there and when I saw you guys were safe, I jumped in the car and came over here to meet you. And it looks like that might have been a good idea." From behind his back he showed them a pile of clothes. "Need these?" he asked.

As they rode over the bridge leading back into town, now fully dressed, the boys sat in the back seat. They looked down at the rapidly flowing water underneath them and PR whispered to James and Julian, "We were idiots!" Nods of agreement were all that needed to be said.

The summer passed and it was now time for Julian to enter high school. PR was a Senior, James a Junior, and Julian was a lowly Freshman. But even though Julian was just in the 9th grade, his sharp tongue and quick temper did not take a back seat to anyone.

His tongue got him into trouble with one of his teachers on one occasion. He was taking a Music Appreciation class and he was called on one day to answer the teacher's question, "Who are Bach, Beethoven and Brahms?" Without hesitation he answered back with his own questions, "What team do they play for and what positions do they play?"

And his feisty temper was on full display a few years later when he was accused of cheating on a test by the teacher. He jumped out of his seat and told her in no uncertain terms, using language a sailor would have been embarrassed by, that he had not cheated. After being sent to the Principal's office and then sent home with a note for his parents to return with him, he was forced to apologize to the teacher for his outburst. He went through the mandatory apology but as the three of them left the room, he muttered under his breath, "But I didn't cheat, you old bag!"

That's not to say that he was not above taking some shortcuts. Julian had developed a strong friendship with a boy named Elliot Speed. Elliot would later go on and play football for the University of Alabama. They were both having a difficult time in a math class their Junior year and it looked like both could possibly fail the class. Their last hope was to pass the final exam.

Speed had a girlfriend who happened to be the teacher's assistant for that class. She was able to get her hands on the final exam questions and she copied it down for the boys. There was only one problem- it was last year's test. But the near tragedy turned out all right. While they had the questions, they still had to study hard enough to figure out the answer to the problems. When the day of the final came, even though they were surprised that they weren't the same questions, their study efforts proved sufficient enough for them to pass the exam.

1943, the year he turned 14, was a year of transition for Julian. Along with entering high school, Julian faced another major decision in his life. Again, he sought the counsel of his long-time mentor, Jere Hardy.

As has been mentioned previously, because of the strong influence of his mother, Julian, along with the other boys, attended church regularly. He read his Bible daily and he prayed often. But he hadn't made the total commitment of accepting Christ as his personal Savior. He knew this was something his mother wanted him to do- the other boys had made their decisions several years before, he just had not felt the pull strongly enough until now. But he wanted to make sure that he was committing for the right reason. One Sunday he sought Mr. Hardy out and asked him to meet him at the local Rexall Drug Store later that day.

At 3 pm on the dot, Mr. Hardy walked in to find Julian already sitting at a booth looking a bit nervous. They shook hands and Mr. Hardy spoke up saying, "Julian, I can tell that you have something heavy on your mind. What is it you want to talk about?"

Julian replied, "I appreciate your taking time to meet with me. I know I'm not in your class anymore since I'm now in the Youth Department at church, but I've always admired you and I didn't have anyone else I could go to. Mom's biased on the subject and Dad, well, I just can't talk to him about this."

"I'm honored you would think of me. Besides, you'll always be one of my boys. Now, what is it?"

Julian lowered his eyes to the table and said, "How do you know when it's the right time to accept Christ into your life?"

"I'll answer that with a question of my own- what does your heart say?"

"It's telling me I need to do it. That I need to walk down the aisle and announce to everybody there that He's my Lord."

"There's your answer. If your heart tells you it's time, then it's time."

With tears in his eyes Julian said, "Thanks, Mr. Hardy. I knew you'd be able to help."

A few Sundays later, on a Sunday where Lanora made sure they stayed for the worship service, Julian accepted Christ. The congregation, en masse, went down to the banks of the Alabama River, the same river he had swum across just a few weeks before, to see Julian be baptized.

By the time Julian reached his Junior year of high school, he was the only son remaining in the household of Peter and Lanora Mock. The two older boys had graduated previously and both had left to join the military.

The year was 1945 and the wars in Europe and the Pacific seemed to be drawing to a close. Germany had surrendered in May of that year after their mad man dictator, Adolph Hitler and his mistress, Eva Braun, had committed suicide just a few weeks before. In early August, the United States dropped an atomic bomb on the Japanese city of Hiroshima followed by another bombing on the city of Nagasaki ultimately ending the war there. Japan would surrender on September 2, 1945.

But the excitement of those events and the thought that American soldiers, pilots, and sailors would finally be returning home after four long years of fighting was tempered by the news that raced across newspaper headlines and radio broadcasts in April of that same year. The country's beloved President, Franklin Delano Roosevelt, had died suddenly from complications of polio that had racked his body. The fact that he had died just a few hundred miles from Selma affected Julian and the entire southeastern part of the country even harder.

The President's health had been declining rapidly, accelerated by the stress of the wars and even though the end seemed in sight, the illness had taken its toll. FDR was taking some down time enjoying the therapeutic waters of Warm Springs, Georgia. On April 12, 1945 he was doing some routine paper work while having his portrait done. He complained of having a severe headache and a few moments later he collapsed and died. The nation mourned his death more than any President since Lincoln. To many, including Julian, the loss was devastating.

But now it was time to move on to better days and to an aspiring athlete, that meant making the varsity baseball team. Julian had already made a name for himself as the hustling manager of both the varsity football and basketball teams. But his real dream was to play under Coach Sims for the Parrish Tigers baseball team.

Tryouts were to be held in March of 1946 and he was ready. He had played summer leagues and performed well showing marked improvement. Already a good hitter, Julian was coached by a man named Maury Arnovich who took extra time to help him with his fielding techniques at second base. By his own admission he did not have great speed or a powerful arm but his reaction to ground balls and exactly where they were going was better than average. Arnovich would continue to work with Julian through his first two summers at Auburn and he gives this man a lot of credit in making him the baseball guru that he would later become. Along with personal skills and techniques, Arnovich would spend time with Julian talking about strategy and the fine points of the game.

On the day of the tryouts, Coach Sims instructed all those who had shown up to go to the position they wanted to play. Julian immediately trotted to second base where he was joined by about a half dozen others. Among those standing there waiting for further instructions was one of his best friends. He was a little surprised to see him go to second because he had always played third base before. But Julian was pretty confident he could beat him out for the position.

When the roster was posted after a couple of grueling days of tryouts, Julian was overjoyed to see his name listed with his new teammates, including that of his good friend. Practices continued for three weeks before the team would play their first game. With each passing day and with each new practice session, Julian's confidence rose and he raced home one day to tell his Dad that he was sure he would be the starter at second.

"Don't be getting too cocky, Buck." his Dad warned. "You still have to work hard and impress Coach Sims."

After batting practice one day, Julian's friend and competitor walked up to him and said, "You've got this locked up. You're hittin' everything in the gaps and you turn the double play a lot better than me. Congratulations!" But when the lineup was posted for the first game, Julian's name was not on the starting lineup card. He was in a daze the entire game and his disappointment continued throughout the season. He only started one game when his friend had the flu and in mop up times when Parrish was either well ahead or way behind. He knew he was better than his friend. For the life of him he could not understand why Coach Sims kept putting his friend in the lineup over him.

He didn't let his discouragement affect his summer league play though. There was nothing in life that he enjoyed more than putting on that uniform.

Julian was always well-liked but he didn't participate in many of the clubs or activities of the school other than sports-related events. His grades were enough to get him by but not especially noteworthy. His time away from school was rather constricted because of his duties around the house and farm. Being the only remaining boy his workload was increased to such an extent that he really didn't have time for anything extracurricular.

As he entered his Senior year, he was confused as to what he was going to do with his life after graduation. Should he enlist in one of the armed forces like his brothers? Should he try his hand at professional baseball? Should he get a job? Or should he go to college? There was no doubt as to which option his Mother wanted him to pursue. All she talked about was him going to school. Somewhere- anywhere.

Even with his passion for the game of baseball, the events of the past year made him think very hard about going out for the team again. A conversation with the boy who had won the job the previous year changed all that indecision. Between classes one day, the boy told him to meet him at lunch- there was something he had to talk to Julian about.

They found an unoccupied table at the back of the cafeteria that was relatively private. Julian tore into his brown bag homemade lunch while the other boy played with the mystery meat on his plate with his fork.

"Are you going out for the team this year?" his friend asked.

Julian replied, "I'm really not sure. If you're playing, I don't see the point unless I try for a different position. You'll be the starter for sure."

"Well, that's what I want to talk to you about. I'm not going out- I'm gonna run track instead." He continued, "See, Julian, I just found out the reason I played ahead of you last year and I'm so mad about it I could spit."

Julian's curiosity was enough to make his head pop. "What're you talkin' about?"

"You know my Dad's the President of the bank in town, don't you?" Julian nodded that he did. "Well, he's also the President of the Selma Baseball Association. That's the group that raises money to help pay for a lot of the equipment that the school gets. Now, don't hate me and don't get mad at Coach Sims but I just discovered that my Dad went to Coach last year and told him that if I didn't start, the team wouldn't get any new equipment. Coach had no choice. He had to start me even though you were so much better."

Julian, not knowing exactly what to say, sat there in total disbelief. The boy looked sadly at him and said, "Please don't hate me. I know you deserve to be the starter. I knew it all last year. I just didn't know why the coach didn't know it but now I understand. That's why I'm gonna run track. Dad can't mess with that."

Julian looked across the table, stuck out his hand and told the boy, "That took guts and I really appreciate what you're doing."

Tryout day rolled around and there was no competition when it came time for the would-be players to line up for second base. Everyone knew that Julian had it won hands down. Julian never said a word to Coach Sims and you could sense that he was relieved about the situation as well.

The Parrish Tigers had a successful year with the Senior second baseman, Julian Mock, leading the team in hitting. Wherever they played, the Tigers usually had scouts and college recruiters in the stands watching Julian.

Graduation day finally arrived and Julian was still as confused as ever about which road in life he should take next. As he proudly walked across the stage when his name was called to accept his diploma, he looked out into the auditorium. He saw both his Mom, smiling broadly, and his Dad, clapping enthusiastically, but he thought it strange that they weren't sitting together. But that was a question for another day.

Julian Rogers Mock finished #59 out of a class of #129.

2nd Inning

"College Days"

"So, Mock- are you with us?" asked one boy. "C'mon, don't be a square." challenged another.

"I don't know guys. Cuttin' class to go to a movie seems pretty silly. What if we get caught? What if Coach finds out?"

"He's not gonna find out and, besides, what's he gonna do? You're his best player- he's not gonna take a chance of losing his last game of the year by punishing you."

"But what if they don't let us graduate?" Julian continued to protest.

"How many lame excuses are you comin' up with, Mock? Listen, either meet here after lunch or don't. It's up to you. But we're going, with or without you."

That's all Julian needed- another tough decision in his life. It wasn't enough that he still couldn't make up his mind about what to do after graduation. Now, two of his friends were putting more pressure on him. But he certainly didn't want them to think he was scared. As he played with his food at lunch, he decided to join them in their little escapade.

The three of them met at the assigned spot and waited for the hall traffic to die down. The only thing that could stand in their way now was for a teacher to see them sneak out of the building. They thought the proverbial jig was up when Mr. Evans, the history teacher saw them lurking around the lockers. Looking over the top of his glasses, he gruffly said, "Gentlemen, I think it is time for you to get to your class." shutting his classroom door without another word.

Randy Blalock

The boys crept by the classrooms that were in session, ducking down under the window in the door so that they wouldn't be seen. They made it to the end of the hall undetected and, once there, they threw open the door making a mad dash for the woods behind the school. Once there, they felt fairly comfortable that their escape had been successful.

The only remaining threat was being seen by one of their parents. Julian knew that his Dad was on his postal route somewhere out in the countryside. When they reached town their eyes searched every possible place one of them could be until they reached the theater.

The boys had not checked what was playing hoping it would be a war movie or maybe a western so, they were disappointed when they looked up at the marquee to see that one of those sappy "Road" movies with Bing Crosby and Bob Hope was playing. In this case it was *The Road to Rio.* But they had come too far in their plan not to go through with every phase of it.

The boys bought their tickets getting a bit of a glare from Mrs. Carter- the same Mrs. Carter who had kicked Julian and his two brothers out of the theater after their prank many years before- still on duty in her ticket window. They found some seats and Julian thought the theater was especially crowded for a weekday afternoon.

They had been in their seats for about thirty minutes. Julian was actually enjoying the movie after all. He had always thought that Bob Hope was funny listening to his radio show with his parents and Dorothy Lamour was very pretty. As usual, Hope and Crosby were trying to wisecrack their way out of trouble when Julian detected some movement from the patrons near the screen. Several were getting up out of their seats in the middle of the picture. It was then that he saw some activity behind the screen.

What followed were the dreaded words that no one caught in a relatively confined space ever wanted to hear. "Fire!" someone yelled. Others joined in, "Fire! Fire!" Julian looked at his two buddies. There was panic all around. The flames were now tearing through the screen and now they were igniting the ceiling and the seats. There were no sprinkler systems at that time so the fire quickly spread. Julian was frozen. His buddies were nowhere to be seen.

He looked behind him to the lobby entrance but the aisles were packed with people clogging that exit route. He thought his best chance would be to run to the front of the theater and try to get out that exit door. He fought his way through the surging crowd to the door. He pushed on the bar to open it, but nothing happened. Either the door was locked or broken, either way he couldn't get out this way. Nevertheless, he banged and pushed on the door until his hands ached from the relentless pounding he exerted on the steel, un-giving door.

He looked behind him and the flames had so totally engulfed the front of the theater that his escape path was now fully blocked. His only hope was that the firemen could find him through the dense smoke that was now making it hard for him to breathe. To help them locate him, he started yelling, "Help! Help! Somebody help me, please!"

Julian groggily awoke to the sounds of his mother's voice and her shaking hands on his shoulder. "Buck, honey. Wake up! Wake up! You're having a terrible nightmare!"

Through foggy eyes, gasping to catch his breath, Julian finally became aware that he was safe in his bed. Coming to the conclusion himself that he had been having a bad dream, he was able to relax and speak. "Wow, Mom. That was a bad one."

Lanora asked if he wanted to talk about it and knowing her reputation as what the people of town called her, a "Dream Diviner", he knew she couldn't or wouldn't rest until he did. Julian's mother had always felt that our dreams told us a lot about what was going in our minds- our struggles, our turmoils, our stresses. Because of that, she had read several books about dream interpretations. Of course, being a religious woman she also felt that dreams were a way that God communicated with us. She was called upon often by neighbors to tell them what their dreams meant. And to Julian's thanks, she knew that the people asking her help didn't think of her as a "kook" or a "crackpot" - just as someone who had an educated gift.

He detailed the story of his dream which was still very fresh in his mind. Lanora listened intently and when he finished, she said, "That's an easy one."

She started her explanation by asking Julian a question, "Where were you before all the bad things began happening?"

Julian answered, "I was in school."

She smiled and said, "Well, there's your answer." Julian's confused look on his face told her that he didn't understand at all.

"School was your safe place. The outside world has dangers you're not ready for just yet. I think this is the Lord's way of telling you to continue your education- to stay in school by going to college." Julian could only smile and think to himself that, perhaps, this interpretation was just a bit contrived since this was what she wanted so much but maybe it was the answer to his decision. There was really no risk. He could always try one of the other options if college didn't work out.

That was it then. He would go to college. Now, the problem would be, where? There was the University of Alabama where his good friend Elliot Speed was going but he also knew several guys who were enrolling at Alabama Polytechnic Institute, better known as Auburn because of the city where it was located.

For the next few weeks Julian researched both schools, along with a few smaller schools, trying to determine the best fit for him. One of his primary considerations, naturally, was the baseball teams of the respective schools. Even though Tuscaloosa was closer, Julian felt he had a better chance of playing at Auburn than at the university and Auburn's tuition was less expensive. Since his Dad was picking up most of that tab (what would turn out to be a total of approximately $2,500 for four years), he thought Auburn was the best choice. He sent off for their enrollment papers, completed and returned them, and was accepted just a few days before he was to report for classes.

Being somewhat late in enrolling, Julian was not left much in the way of housing options. The best and least expensive facility that was left was an old Victorian-style two-story house that had been converted to dorm rooms.

The bottom floor was a large entrance area with a dining room and kitchen making up the rest of the space downstairs. There was also a small bedroom where the "dorm mom" lived.

The second floor consisted of four bedrooms that were able to hold up to four students. Those potential sixteen students had to share one bathroom. One bathroom with one tub, one sink, and one toilet. Along with bathing, the tub was used for laundry purposes since the students had to do their own laundry.

This, however, and much to the dismay of Julian and his fellow roommates, was not a problem with one of the young men he shared a room with. The boy came from a very poor family and he arrived with only two sets of clothes- two shirts, two pair of overalls, two pair of socks, one pair of scuffed-up shoes and two sets of underwear. He would wear one set of clothes for an entire week and, to conserve soap, would take his weekly bath with them on. This form of cleansing left much to be desired in the way of odor-prevention so, Julian and the other boys would tie his soiled clothes to the end of a long pole and hang them out the window in the hopes they would air out a little. Julian remembers that it never fully removed the stench.

To help pay for items such as room and board, books, and other necessary expenses beyond tuition, Julian took on several jobs. This also gave him a little extra spending money. He refereed youth basketball and football games and, during Auburn's football season, he sold seat cushions at home games. He remembers making up to $25/game on big games.

A few weeks into the semester, a notice was posted announcing that all those interested in playing baseball for the school should report to the gym for an introductory meeting. There looked to be about 90-100 young men in the auditorium that day, but many of them were returning players who would, more than likely, automatically make the team. Julian knew that he faced a big challenge since some of the best ball players in the state of Alabama were in that room. He also knew that freshmen were not eligible to play varsity until their sophomore year, but he still wanted to make a good impression on Auburn's coach, John Williamson.

After the meeting in which Coach Williamson laid down some basic rules as well as posting the date for tryouts, a few of the guys, including Julian, were hanging around getting to know each other better. Julian was standing with a group as he noticed Coach Williamson approaching them.

"You're that Mock kid from Selma, aren't ya?" he asked.

"Yes, sir. I'm surprised you know who I am."

"Well, Coach Sims wrote me that you were coming to Auburn and that I ought to make sure you play ball for us. Are you as good as he says you are?" the coach asked.

"Sir, I don't know. How good did he say I was?"

The coach laughed and said, "He said you were one of the best pure hitters he'd ever seen and I have a lot of respect for what Comer says." The coach continued, "But I know you've basically been a second baseman and there's gonna be a lot of strong competition for that spot. Ever played any other position?"

"No, sir, but I'd be willing to try anything. I just want to play."

"Well, I'll look forward to seeing you this spring. You know, of course, that you can't play with the big boys till next year but we'll field a freshman team and that'll give you some time to settle in to college play- it's a lot different from high school."

Julian left that meeting elated and ready to play. It was a long time till spring but he'd be ready when the time came.

Julian was walking on campus enjoying a beautiful fall day. He was finished with classes for the day so he was planning to drop by the campus post office to see if he had any mail. He frequently got mail from his mother mainly saying how much she missed him and he once even got a letter from James which surprised him greatly.

He entered the office and said hi to the young coed behind the window. He asked if he had any mail and she searched and found one piece of mail. He recognized the handwriting immediately and thought it strange to receive a letter from this person but decided to wait until he got back to his room to open and read it.

As he sat down on his bed, he tore the envelope and began reading. The letter was short and succinct. It read:

> *Dear Buck*
> *I hope this letter finds you well and that you are doing well with your studies. If at all possible, please try to come home this weekend. We have not gone fishing in a long time and I would like for us to do that. If you cannot make it, I will understand but if you can get a ride, I will pick you up at 11 am at the house this Saturday. Hope to see you then.*
> *Dad*

"Pick me up at the house?" Julian said out loud. "Why will he pick me up? Won't he already be there?"

Julian couldn't imagine what the urgency (*try to come home this weekend*) and the importance of going fishing could be. The rest of the days of the week dragged by but Saturday morning finally arrived. His friend picked him up at 7 am giving more than enough time to get to Selma by 11.

When Julian entered the house, his mother ran to him, threw her arms around him, and began crying. This caught Julian off guard since his mother was, generally, a composed, almost stoic, lady. They talked for awhile until they heard a car pull into the yard. Hearing the noise, Lanora ran off into the bedroom closing the door behind her.

Peter greeted Julian with a warm embrace, something else that was totally out of character for him. They spoke very little, other than general conversational topics, during the ride to the lake Peter had chosen for them to fish. They got their gear out of the trunk of the car and slid down the bank to a little boat that Peter had borrowed for the occasion.

"Glad you could make it. I know it was short notice and I didn't know if you had a big test to study for but I'm glad you came."

"Sure, Dad. It was good to get away from that cramped dorm room for the weekend."

They pushed the boat off from the bank and paddled out a few hundred yards before settling into a spot Peter thought good. As they baited their hooks and threw out their lines, there was silence between them. Peter finally broke the silence.

"There's a couple of things I want to talk to you about." He said.

"Fire away!" Julian replied, trying to ease what seemed to him to be a heavy mood.

"Have you decided what your major is going to be?" Peter asked.

"I really don't have to declare for awhile yet so I haven't given it a great deal of thought, but I guess I'm leaning towards a Business Degree."

"That's what I thought you'd say and it makes a lot of sense, Buck, but I don't think that's the right thing for you to do." Julian continued to watch his line looking for signs of a bite waiting for his Dad to continue. "You see, I've seen the way you've loved sports since you were a little boy. I've seen the way you've studied the game of baseball- not just play it but really study it. I've watched you read everything you could get your hands on about football and basketball and even though you weren't really tall enough or big enough to play them, you know as much about how they are played than those who do play. Buck, I think you need to be a coach."

This was definitely something he had thought about but to hear his Dad say it reinforced his thinking on the matter. He replied, "I have given that a lot of thought. It'd be great to coach like Coach Sims. Maybe I will choose Phys Ed as my major. And if I'm going to coach, I'd like to teach, too."

More silence hovered for a few moments until Peter spoke again. "There's one more thing I need to tell you and this will be the most difficult thing I've ever told you in my life. Put your pole down, son. I need you to really listen to me."

"Buck, your mother and I are getting a divorce. You don't need to know why, you just need to know that we are."

"The hell I don't!" Julian hollered.

"Buck, I know you're upset but I'm still your father and I won't be cussed or yelled at. Do you hear me?"

"Yes, sir. But I don't understand."

"It's hard to explain. Maybe it's because you boys are grown and out of the house- we've just grown apart."

"Do PR and Buddy know?" Julian asked.

"Yeah! Your Mom called them a few weeks back but we both thought it was best to tell you in person. And don't you worry a thing about school. I'll still pay for yer schoolin'. "

With tears in his eyes, Julian asked, "Do you still love Mom?"

"I'll always love her, Buck but sometimes a marriage needs more than love. Maybe you'll understand that better one day."

"I doubt it." Julian admitted.

They sat there, both looking into the water, not knowing what to say next until Julian said, "Dad. I don't feel much like fishing. Could you take me home? I think I need to be with Mom." His Dad said only one word- "Sure." Not a word was spoken between them on the drive back to the house. When Peter stopped the car in front, he held out his hand. Julian gripped it firmly and said, "Are you okay?" Julian nodded. Peter added, "You're a helluva kid, Buck. A hellava kid."

Julian entered the house and saw his mother standing over the kitchen sink. Without a word, he walked to her and put his arms tightly around her. They both started crying.

The freshman year sped by quickly. Julian managed to keep his grades adequate, not Dean's List status to be certain, but adequate. Baseball season arrived and Coach Williamson made sure there was a spot for him on the roster. As promised, the freshman team played several games against other opponents, even playing against some varsity competition of some smaller schools. But most of their work came against Auburn's varsity to simulate game-play situations.

Julian performed well in real games and against the varsity. He continued to play second base and in one game against the University of Tennessee's freshman team, he went 5x5 in a game they routed. The Auburn newspaper mentioned him in an article stating that because of Julian and a couple of other outstanding freshmen, things looked good for the school's baseball chances in the coming years.

Spring, 1949. It was now time for tryouts for the varsity. Julian thought he had a good chance of making the team, but he was still nervous as the day approached. Julian was joined by about thirty other young men with aspirations of wearing the Auburn uniform and much like his high school tryouts, Coach Williamson blew his whistle to get their attention and told them that the next time they heard the whistle they were to go to the position they wanted to play. But first, they were to pair up and play catch to warm up their arms.

Before Julian could find one of his buddies from the previous year's freshman team, a bear of a man came over to him, threw his arm around Julian's shoulder and told him to grab a ball. There was no way he was going to argue with this hulk so he did as he was told.

"I've heard about you, squirt!" he said. Julian was not about to take offense at the slight since, compared to him he was. "My name's Erskine, but my friends call me Erk. You can call me Mr. Russell." Erk Russell laughed heartily at his own joke.

For those of you readers who have followed the University of Georgia or Georgia Southern football fortunes over the past forty years, you will recognize the name immediately. To those that may not know him, Erk Russell was the Defensive Coordinator under fellow Auburn alum, Vince Dooley, during Georgia's glory years of the 70's and in 1980 he helped them win a National Championship. After leaving Georgia in 1981 to become the head coach at Georgia Southern, he helped establish the football program leading them to three national championships of their own.

Russell not only played football at Auburn but basketball and baseball as well. He would be the starting first baseman for the team in this his senior season.

They continued to chat as they threw to each other and Julian knew immediately he had made a new friend. Fate was about to throw another new friendship directly in his path.

The shrill sound of the whistle caught everyone's attention and Julian trotted to second base. The line was rather long- long enough that it met up with the line for those who wished to play shortstop. Julian stood next to a player who looked a bit older than the rest of the group. He held his hand out and introduced himself, "Hi! I'm Red Whitsett."

Waiting their respective turns to field some balls at their respective positions, Julian was able to find out that Red was getting a late start on college because he had served in the military. He would later discover that Red had been wounded and that injury would result in him having to curtail his playing days when he reinjured his leg later that season. Red would have a very important role in Julian's life a few years later but from that moment on, they became very close friends.

Julian looked good at second that day but he really showed his talents taking batting practice where, in his words, "I absolutely tore the cover off the ball. There was no way the coach could keep me off the team." His confidence was proven to be correct a few days later when the roster was posted. He called his mom with the news that night adding, "Be sure and tell Dad, won't you?"

Opening day arrived and Julian was so proud to put on his #9 uniform. Only problem was, "It came nowhere near fitting. I had a 29" waist with 36" pants. I spent most of my time holding my pants up. I couldn't have run to first without them falling down around my knees." So maybe it was a good thing that he was not in the starting lineup that first day.

But when the second game arrived and he was still not in the lineup, he began worrying. He had had time to get his uniform altered so he was more comfortable now and ready to play. He was called on late in the game to pinch hit and delivered with a solid, run scoring single and figured he'd get the call next time since the guy playing second ahead of him had not gotten a hit as yet. Another pinch hit, this time a double, in the next game gave him confidence that, surely, he would start next time. But, no- his name still did not appear.

After that game he approached Coach Williamson and asked if he was doing something wrong. "I'm doing pretty good in practices and I'm 2x2 in games so far. What've I gotta do?"

Williamson looked him in the eye and told him, "I told you it was gonna be tough at second base. Ralph's here on scholarship and I'm under pressure to play him. I explained that you might need to move to another position. Ready to give something else a try?"

"Yes, sir. Where you want me to go? I told you I'd do and play anywhere."

"Good. Tomorrow at practice you start workin' in left field. We'll see how that works out."

So, after years of playing nothing but second base, Julian Mock became an outfielder. He would start every game there in left field the remainder of his sophomore season and his entire junior year before moving to centerfield for his senior year. Constantly trying to improve his skills, he would play semi-pro ball during the summers earning additional spending money for himself.

One of the perks of being a letterman was being a part of a select group known as the A Club. He was accepted into the organization after his sophomore year but like all newcomers, it was not official until he made it through a rigorous initiation ritual.

Julian says that it was the most grueling, humiliating experience of his life, taking not just one night, but an entire week of hazing. He recalls two specific events as being the worse.

"For the entire week of initiation, we played what was referred to as 'Rotten Fruit and Vegetable Baseball.' The game would be played each day at noon in the main quad and would draw a large crowd of students as spectators. The pitcher would throw a piece of rotten fruit or vegetable at the batter who would attempt to hit it. Whether he did or not he would run to first base, all the while being pelted by other forms of rotten fruit or vegetation, some the size of cantaloupes which would hurt like the dickens. By the end of the 'game', you'd be covered and stained and the odor would penetrate all the way to the skin. It would take several baths to get the stains and smell off."

The second degrading experience he recalled was the Midnight Hike. "You'd be rousted out of your bed at midnight and, in nothing but your underwear, you'd set out on a five-mile hike. Along the way, we'd have to stop where we'd get covered in honey or have flour thrown on us. If we heard someone yell, 'flop it', we'd have to lie down in the dirt of the road and roll around. But the worst part was being taken to a cow pasture where we had to crawl for hundreds of yards on our bellies. You can just imagine what we had to crawl through."

After surviving initiation, however, some positives things came the way of the members of the A Club. One of the sororities on campus would have "Date Night with the A Club" each year. A member of the sorority would draw the name of an A Club member and they would go out on a date. The sorority was known for its beautiful young ladies so this, for many of the A Club, was a night they looked forward to.

Julian's name was drawn by a young lady that he described as "a real looker." It was a night that he really looked forward to.

By this time, his junior year, Julian had moved out of the original dorm where he had lived his first two years and moved into a small apartment that he and his one roommate shared. They rented the apartment from an elderly couple that left them alone unless they got too loud. Julian's new roommate came from a relatively wealthy family from Decatur, Alabama and after discovering that Julian had been lucky enough to have the "knockout" as his date, the roommate surprised him by giving him the use of his car for the night of the date.

On the night in question as Julian left to pick up the girl at the sorority house, the roommate told him, "It's got a full tank of gas" and with a wink of his eye, "and I don't want to see you back here until tomorrow morning."

When he arrived at the house, he politely asked for the girl in question. Expecting to see her come down the steps, he was a bit taken back when another girl, a far less attractive girl, in fact as he recalls, "a real Plain Jane" came down instead. He found out later that the sorority, knowing that none of the men of the A Club would want to go out with this less attractive sister, substituted the other girls' name. Julian had just gotten the short straw as it were. Ever the gentleman, however, and knowing that his momma would be severely upset with him if she ever found out he did not treat this young lady with politeness and civility, he sat down with her in the parlor and they talked for over an hour. Needless to say, Julian made it back to his room well before dawn's early light.

The years had passed by quickly. Between the arduous study, the time spent working jobs so that he could earn a little money to help with his expenses, and baseball, his senior year was now upon him. Since assuming his new outfield position, Julian had established himself as one of the best, if not the best, hitters on the team. His defensive skills had improved, too. He was now asked by the new coach, Dick McGowan, to move to centerfield and Julian gladly accepted his new role.

And before the season was to start, Julian was honored by his teammates who elected him to be the Co-Captain of the team. He was sharing this honor with a boy named Ray Dean who would later go on to coach at Roosevelt High School in Atlanta.

Julian had an outstanding senior season. He remembers two particular highlights that occurred that season.

The first took place against the University of Florida in Gainesville. Julian tells it like this: "Florida had an unusual-shaped field. The fence was fairly standard down the lines but it abruptly went way out in right center and dead center was about 450'. Florida had a catcher by the name of Haywood Sullivan who would later become a part owner of the Boston Red Sox. Haywood was known to be a talker and because the wind was blowing out to right center that day, he told me as I came up to bat in the first inning, 'Mock, you might even hit one deep today.' I knew that the smart-aleck comment was made to throw me off and get me swinging for the fences which was the worse thing I could do. Course it was probably a slap at my lack of size, too. Anyway, on the second pitch, I hit the ball as solidly as I had ever hit one in my life. It took off and so did I cause I figured I had hit it in the gap. They had wooden fences and the ball must have hit between the planks. It caromed off that fence like a pinball and both outfielders overran the ball. Now, I wasn't fast, by any means, but by the time they got to the ball, I was between second and third. I was amazed when I looked up to see the third base coach waving me home. I crossed the plate standing up with the first home run of my career- an inside-the-parker, but a home run, nevertheless. After scoring I looked back at Sullivan and said, 'Guess you were right!'"

His second highlight came against Auburn's arch rival, Alabama, and their star pitcher, Frank Lary. Lary was a hard-throwing right hander who would later go on to have a nice major league career, mainly with the Detroit Tigers. Frank Lary was known as "The Yankee Killer" for his uncanny success against that one particular team. It should be noted that Lary pitched at a time when the Yankees were the most-feared team in all of baseball. From 1955-1961, Lary had a record of 27-10 against the Yankees while having a .500 record against the rest of the league.

But on this day in 1951 he couldn't get the scrappy Auburn centerfielder out to save his life. Julian remembers: "Lary had a wicked fast ball but for some reason, he led me off with a changeup. I laced it back up the middle for a base hit. My second time up he must have thought I had gotten lucky cause he threw me another changeup. Bam! Up the middle for another hit. My third time, he finally threw me a fastball and I got enough of it to spray it into left field for another hit. 3x3 against anybody was a pretty good day but against Frank Lary, it was a great day. Of course, we got beat 18-3."

The final highlight was a defensive play he made one day that had a humorous side to it. The centerfielder is supposed to take charge of any fly ball he can get to but, perhaps, Julian overstepped that rule one day. The opponent hit a high fly that kept drifting and drifting to his left. Being an aggressive player in all aspects of the game, Julian called off the right fielder yelling, "I got it! I got it!" When he made the catch, he realized that he was all the way in right field with the right fielder standing five feet away with his hands on his hips as if to say, "What the heck are you doing?"

Julian trots back to center somewhat sheepishly. The next batter lofts a foul ball down the right field line well out of play and a voice from the stands calls out, "Hey, Mock. What's the matter? Aren't you going to get that one, too?"

Julian led the team in hitting that year finishing with a .353 average. One of the local newspapers summed it up best by saying: *Julian Mock, Tiger outfielder, may be the smallest player in the SEC but his batting average is one of the biggest. Professional baseball scouts tend to overlook the little boys, but scouts will learn that Mock seldom overlooks a good pitch. The sharp-eyed Selma native leads Auburn's hitting brigade with a slightly under .400 average.*

With graduation, it was now time to move on to another phase of life- this one with life-changing opportunities.

3rd Inning

"Military and Miss Dot"

In June, 1950, the army of North Korea, supplied and supported by the Soviet Union, invaded South Korea. The "police action" took on international proportions when the United Nations, with the principal participant being the United States, joined the conflict on the side of South Korea. Based on this action, the People's Republic of China joined the conflict on the side of the North Koreans.

In June, 1951, the conflict, now called The Korean War, was going strong but Julian Mock had prepared for his part in serving his country. Instead of playing summer league baseball, as he usually had, Julian spent the summer between his junior and senior college years attending summer ROTC camp. This, along with his ROTC classes and training while attending Auburn, would allow him to enter the service as a commissioned 2nd Lieutenant. He had chosen the Air Force as his branch of service. After graduation, he had spent a few weeks in Selma before he was to report to Lawson Field at Ft. Benning, Georgia in July, 1951.

As one might expect, when it came time for him to leave, there were plenty of tears from his mother and proud embraces from his father. The divorce had become final years before but there was still tension when both were in the same room so, to alleviate that, Julian made concentrated efforts to see them separately. His dad had remarried and Julian did the best he could to accept the woman that was now in his dad's life.

As all mothers do when their sons leave home, Lanora made him promise to write her and Julian, naturally, told her he would.

Upon arrival, Julian, as 2nd Lieutenant, was appointed Adjutant. In essence, he was second in command of the entire base. He was always able to make friends easily so even though he was always giving orders, the men liked him. He also got along, generally, with his superiors which would benefit him greatly down the road.

He was so well liked by the men under him that they got his permission before they pulled a prank on a gullible young boy from Arkansas. While he didn't participate himself in the prank, he did give them his blessing since there was no physical harm that was being done. It was just a way for the men to release a little steam from the boredom of training they usually experienced.

The Korean War was raging half way round the world but that did not keep the alarmists silent with their continued warnings that the US could be attacked at any time. Radio and the new medium that was sweeping the country, television, kept the nation up to date with what was going on in Korea. Each day brought more news of battles and mounting casualties. For some, the news was more terrifying than others.

The boy from Arkansas, let's call him Joe, had come from the Ozarks and in every sense of the word could be called a hillbilly. He was naïve, relatively uneducated, and the butt of most of the jokes being played in the barracks. But he took all of the kidding in stride, not realizing that the others were making fun of him and taking advantage of his good nature. Another boy in the company was from Illinois, but his parents were Korean and he could speak the language fluently. He would be the star of the prank.

On the night of the prank, Joe was sent out on an errand. In the dark of the night, Joe was accosted by several of his barrack mates, blindfolded, tied up, and led back to a supply room where he was held. One of the men was good with electronics so he had been able to rig a fake broadcast.

"Attention, America! Our nation is under attack! We have had reports that several Korean battleships have been sighted off the coast of North Carolina and that a contingent of heavily armed Korean soldiers are making their way to Ft. Bragg to overtake that facility. Be on the alert!"

Joe could hear the door open to where he was being held. The Korean boy from Illinois began barking out orders. Others in the room began scurrying around and mumbling in fake Korean gibberish. Knowing that he had been captured by this invading army, Joe began doing what any good soldier, sailor, or pilot was trained to do. He started yelling his name, rank, and serial number. Over and over he called these out; all to the amusement of those involved.

At some point during his interrogation, his bindings were loosed. The "North Koreans" left the room and he realized he could untie himself and take his blindfold off. He was able to escape and once he thought himself safe, he ran to the first person he saw and reported his abduction. They, of course, had no idea of what he was talking about. The next day he was full of excitement as he told everyone he could how he had escaped from the enemy.

But baseball was never far away from Julian. He was player/manager of the base team and one day in October, 1951 while doing paperwork in the base headquarters, he was able to hear the radio broadcast of one of the most significant games ever played in Major League Baseball. 2nd Lieutenant Julian Mock heard the "Shot Heard Round the World."

The New York Giants and Brooklyn Dodgers, bitter rivals during any situation, were involved in a monumental battle for the National League pennant in 1951. In mid-August the Giants were as much as 13.5 games behind the league-leading Dodgers, only to win 37 out of their last 44 games to tie the Dodgers on the final day of the season.

A best two out of three game series would decide who would go on to play the other inner-city rival, the New York Yankees, in the World Series. The Giants won the first game on a home run by Bobby Thomson off Dodger pitcher, Ralph Branca. Remember both of those names. The Dodgers easily won the second game setting up a winner-take-all third game.

The Dodgers took a 4-1 lead into the bottom of the ninth until Dodger starting pitcher, Don Newcombe, began to falter. The Giants rallied and made the score 4-2 with runners on second and third. The manager then brought in Branca from the bullpen to face, guess who? Bobby Thomson. A young rookie by the name of Willie Mays waited in the on-deck circle.

As Thomson came to the plate, Lt. Mock remembers telling one of his fellow officers, "He's gonna knock it out of the park and the Giants are gonna win."

Julian should have bet a lot of money on that prediction. They heard the Giants' announcer, Russ Hodges say on Armed Forces Radio: "There's a long drive. It's gonna be...I believe. The Giants win the pennant! The Giants win the pennant! The Giants win the pennant! They're going crazy! I don't believe it! They're picking Bobby Thomson up on their shoulders and carrying him off the field."

As stated previously, he was made the player/manager for the base baseball team but his ability to get along with his superiors really came to his advantage while at Lawson. The Base Commander found out that Julian was a good athlete and asked him to play golf with him one day. Before long, the commander and he were going out most every day that the weather allowed to play as many as 36 holes at the nearby course.

Julian said he eased up on him that first day and let him win. He noticed that he could outdrive the officer so instead of using his driver, he hit his drives with a 3-wood. And he would purposely miss a few putts here and there. But when they started playing for money, Julian's skills dramatically improved, much to the dismay of the CO.

Early in 1952, Julian was transferred to Pope Air Force Base at Ft. Bragg, North Carolina. He was assigned to the Radio Relay Division as an Administrative Assistant in the paratrooper's unit. To this point in his life, Julian had never been in a plane. He admits to being terrified that he would have to learn to jump from a plane but that, luckily for him, never transpired. In fact, he said he rarely even travelled in a plane during his entire time in the service. He was just responsible for the communication between the ground and the aircraft.

But on March 5, 1952, an event occurred that would change his life forever. Julian was on duty in the radio room when one of the enlisted men came rushing into the room shouting, "Lt. Mock! Lt. Mock!"

"What is it, corporal, and have you forgotten how to salute?"

"Sorry, sir." as he gave a sharp salute, "I was excited. I just thought you'd want to know about this as soon as possible."

"Know what, corporal?"

"I was down at the commander's headquarters and a new WAF has just reported for duty. I heard her say that she was from Alabama and I just figured you'd want to know. Besides, she's a real looker!"

"Bring the jeep around. I think I need to welcome her to the base." Julian ordered.

The trip did not take long and as Julian stepped out of the jeep, he made sure his shirt was tucked in, the creases of his pants were straight, and his shoes shined to perfection. He opened the door and gazed for the first time on Dorothy Lucille Strange. He was smitten immediately. He would later say that "It took Dot a couple of months to know that I was the one for her. It took me three minutes."

Julian politely introduced himself and volunteered to be her escort around the base. "I'll be glad to show you around, ma'am. You know, this is a pretty big place and it would be easy for a lady to get lost. Let me help you get acclimated." Dorothy smiled and agreed to let him give her a guided tour.

Dorothy, or Miss Dot as she is lovingly referred to now, was born in the rural mill town of Sylacauga, Alabama. Her family was poor, as most families in town were, but their existence was made more difficult by problems her father suffered. She was good in school and was never at a loss for boyfriends because of her beauty.

In high school she was a majorette but helped in the support of her family by working in the local mill. Working there, she caught the eye of the owner of the mill who convinced her she should go into modeling.

She had several modeling assignments with one of them providing her with partial financial aid to attend college. She attended the University of Alabama for a short period but felt that she didn't fit in and dropped out. Walking down the street one day she saw a recruitment office and decided to go in. Shortly thereafter, she enlisted in the WAF (Women's Air Force) and was assigned to Pope.

As she recalls: "I was told that there were openings at bases in California and since I had never been out of Alabama much I was hoping I would get assigned there. Pope was definitely not my first choice but I guess it worked out all right." That appears to be an understatement since they celebrated their 62nd year of marriage last year.

Julian and Dot's first date was, you guessed it, a baseball game. The base team was playing a group of semi-pro players from the area and Julian wanted to impress her. The best way to do that, he thought, was to play well, but he also thought that he better give up his chewing tobacco for, at least, that game.

The fact that Dot was an enlisted service woman and Julian was an officer proved to be difficult to their relationship on some occasions. One of Julian's duties on the base was that of Pay Master. He was responsible for reviewing and distributing pay to everyone stationed at the base including the women serving there.

One of Dot's duties was to pick up the respective pay for the women stationed there. The trouble with that, however, was that if she came into contact with, now 1st Lieutenant Julian Mock, while on duty, she would have to salute him. She says of that probability, "I'd kiss him but there was no way I was going to salute him."

To get around this potential problem she would make sure that Julian was not in the office when it was time for her to pick up the pay. She would either have someone who worked with Julian in the office call her to alert her he was out or she would go when she knew he was out playing golf or pool with the commander.

To Julian, the next step in their relationship was a foregone conclusion. He bought a ring and planned to propose while on their next date.

He requisitioned a vehicle from the car pool and picked her up at her barracks for the drive into town to see a movie.

They drove into nearby Fayetteville, North Carolina, got some dinner before going to see *Pat and Mike* starring Spencer Tracy and Kathryn Hepburn and featuring, in his first credited movie role, tough-guy Charles Bronson. Julian remembers being more nervous before getting up the nerve to pop the question than during any game situation he had ever been. But the hard-to-convince girl from Sylacauga said yes and the small-town boy from Selma became the "happiest fella in the entire US Air Force."

They were married on July 5, 1952 in a small ceremony on the base. They honeymooned in Panama City and travelled back to Alabama to visit both sets of relatives before heading back to North Carolina to finish their service time.

The newlyweds, however, had a big problem to overcome. A few weeks prior to their wedding, Lt. Mock had gotten into an argument with a major. The major was so incensed by the altercation that he had the young lieutenant transferred to Greenville, South Carolina. So, for the first month of their marriage, Julian would have to commute from Greenville to Pope Field, a distance of about 270 miles, long before the interstate system was in place.

Julian recalls: "I came up every weekend and we stayed in a motel. I would leave at 11:00 pm on Sunday night and drive all night. One night I got so sleepy that I pulled over on the main street of whatever little South Carolina town I was in and got back in the back seat to catch a few minutes of sleep. When I woke up it was the first light of day. People were stopping at the car and looking at me strangely trying to figure out what I was doing sleeping in the middle of town. I made it to my base at 7 am and made it to work on time At 8 am. I napped a little that morning because I had to be ready to shoot pool with my CO all afternoon. Golf had changed to pool. Tough duty, right? I always won. I had had good training as a teenager at the YMCA pool table."

He continues: "The squadron that I was in was the same Group that Dot worked in when I was at Pope. She was the CO's secretary at Pope and he got tired of her moping around all the time. He asked her one day what the problem was and when she told him what had happened and that I was now in Greenville, he reacted quickly. The next day, I was back in North Carolina. That same week that I reported back to Pope, we got an apartment in Fayetteville."

The differences in rank continued to be problematic for them, particularly for Dot as she had to deal with being an enlisted wife of an officer. She was, for example, expected to attend the Officer's Wives Club meetings and socials which were never a pleasant experience for her. Many of the other wives would snub her if not outright ignore her but the parties at the Officer's Club proved to be even more of a problem for her.

Dot especially remembers one particular party. She and Julian arrived at the Club but they soon became separated. Standing by herself, Dot saw her superior WAF officer approaching her. Even though neither of them was in uniform, Dot knew the proper protocol and saluted her as she neared. The CO roughly pulled Dot's arm down and berated her for her action. She questioned why Dot was there and, to put it simply, told her that as an enlisted woman she had no place there, wife of an officer or not. The chastisement continued for several minutes and even though Dot was, and is, a strong woman, she was brought near to tears.

She refused to let Julian know anything about the incident but word had gotten back, somehow, to the Colonel. Enraged by the woman's actions, it was soon noticeable that the female officer was never seen on that base again.

1953 began with a literal boom as President Harry Truman announced the development of the hydrogen bomb. Later that month the country saw a new President, Dwight D. Eisenhower inaugurated and on January 19th, over 68% of all televisions in the country were tuned in to watch *I Love Lucy*. The episode featured the birth of Lucy's, played by Lucille Ball and Desi's, played by her husband Desi Arnaz son.

In February, Walt Disney's feature length film, *Peter Pan* was released and at the University of Cambridge the discovery of the structure of the DNA molecule was announced.

March saw the death of Russian dictator Joseph Stalin. But medical history was announced, history that would affect millions of American children later that year, when Jonas Salk announced the development of the first successful polio vaccine.

In April, Ian Fleming published the first James Bond thriller, *Casino Royale* and victory by the UN forces around the 38th Parallel in Korea were the first signs that the fighting there would soon be over.

From Here to Eternity won the Best Picture Oscar. William Holden for *Stalag 17* and Audrey Hepburn for *Sabrina* won Best Actor and Actress.

And in the world of sports, the Detroit Lions won the NFL Championship by defeating the Cleveland Browns; the Montreal Canadiens won the Stanley Cup; Ben Hogan won the Masters; and Indiana defeated Kansas in the NCAA Men's Basketball Championship.

For Julian and Dot Mock, discharge loomed on the horizon. They had both given some thought to making the military a career but a phone call Julian made in May, 1952 changed that.

Julian had often said that if he was not married when his military service was over, he would try his hand at playing baseball professionally. That, of course, was no longer the case as he and Dot would soon celebrate their first year of marriage in July. He realized he needed to find permanent employment. He had kept in touch with his good friend from his Auburn days, Red Whitsett. Red was now coaching in Atlanta at Grady High School with their mutual buddy, Erk Russell. Julian sought help from Red and the wheels were set in motion.

Red was aware that there was a coaching position open at Southwest High School in Atlanta if Julian was interested. Julian did as much as he could via long distance and would travel down to Atlanta on weekends for interviews. He got the job and after his discharge in July, 1953, he began his coaching career in August. Dot's discharge would not come until September so, Julian came ahead to set up their first apartment- a cozy one-bedroom bungalow on Gordon Road. The legend of Coach Julian Mock was about to begin.

4th Inning

"The Murphy Years"

Julian Mock joined the coaching staff of Southwest High School in August, 1953. Along with his coaching duties, he taught both English and World History. The school had just been opened a few years prior and its athletic programs were still getting established. Nevertheless, the school was blessed with some good athletes and they quickly became a contender in the highly-competitive arena of City of Atlanta athletics.

One of his players from that era, Joe Stovall, Class of 1957, said of Julian: "I played for Coach Mock in 1955 and 1956 and in those two short years he made quite an influence on my life." Stovall remembers that he (Mock) would often take time between classes to talk to those congregating in the halls. And as Stovall recalls, "He wasn't getting on to us trying to get us back in class. He was trying to learn who we were and if we played ball for him, he was always ready to talk sports." Stovall went on, "And while he talked, he would be in a squatting position. When we would comment on how long he could stay in a squat, he would quickly tell us, 'This is nothing. You should see how long my daddy could squat.'"

Being the new guy, Coach Mock was not able to coach any varsity competition that first year but he was named "B" Team coach for football, basketball, and baseball. He remained the "B" Team football and basketball coach the three years he was there but was elevated to be the head varsity baseball coach for 1955 and 1956. After inheriting a team that had lost just about everyone from the previous year due to graduation, he was able to get the best out of his players in 1955 and led them to a 5-5 record.

His talent and skill as a coach was definitely seen the following year as he led Southwest to a 7-3 record and a chance to play for the City of Atlanta Championship series against Northside in 1956. They would lose that series but because of their performance, Julian was named the All-Star Coach for the City of Atlanta team that year. Under his leadership, the City of Atlanta All-Stars defeated the Metro Atlanta All-Stars.

Another one of his players, Leon Norton, called Coach Mock, "a hard-nosed guy who expected nothing less than your best if you were going to play for him." He also remembers the wad of tobacco that was always in Coach Mock's cheek as he coached, a tradition that was carried on to his days at Murphy in memorable ways.

The honor of being named All-Star coach was the first of many future awards that would come his way, but an event that had taken place the previous year was the best honor that Julian had received to that point in his life.

Julian worked long, hard hours rarely getting home before 8: 00 pm but even though Dot was a working lady herself, she always had a hot supper waiting for him when he got home. He arrived home one night in February, 1955 after coaching his B team basketball squad at Southwest. He greeted Dot with a kiss and went into their small dining area. Dot would always wait to have her dinner with him no matter how late it might be so that they could have some time together discussing the good and the bad of their respective days. Dot would say, "Julian always made sure that he asked me about my day. He was never so self-centered that he thought what he was doing was the only thing that mattered."

On this particular night as Julian sat down at the compact dinette table, he noticed that there was a third place setting laid out. For a few moments he let it pass thinking it was just a mistake. Finally, he asked Dot, "Are we expecting somebody else for dinner?"

"Not for a few months, yet." she responded.

"A few months? Who is it and why is the plate out now?"

Dot smiled at his naivety. She got up, went to another room, and came back with something behind her back. She placed a baby bottle next to the plate. Julian just stared at it until the realization of what she was trying to tell him sank in. "Does this mean what I think it means?" he asked.

"Yes. Are you happy?"

He answered her by jumping out of his chair giving her a big hug and lifting her off the ground in excitement. Terry Leigh Mock was born on September 20, 1955 marking the first of three times he would receive the honor of being called "Daddy."

After settling into their living quarters on Gordon Road, Dot decided she wanted to get her degree. The couple realized that they could use the additional income Dot could earn as a college graduate because they had taken a fairly sizable cut in pay when they left the military. Julian said, "We were making a combined military salary of about $700 per month which was good money in those days. After I was discharged, my beginning salary as a teacher and coach at Southwest was $350 a month. It took Dot a little while to find a job in Atlanta but even when she did, our total income was a lot less than it had been while we were in the service." Dot was able to attend school on the GI Bill and she enrolled at Georgia State which, in those years, was an extension of UGA. Julian, as well, continued his education by obtaining his Masters in Physical Education in 1956 after attending summer school at both Auburn and Georgia State.

Another phone call, this one initiated by Julian, brought about a job change that would affect, not only his life, but the lives of hundreds of students during the next eight years at Murphy High School in Atlanta, Georgia.

J. C. Murphy High School opened its doors to its Clifton Street location in southeast Atlanta in 1948. For a few years prior it had existed in a different location on Memorial Drive before the new building was built. Murphy served as the high school for several elementary schools in that area: Burgess, Whiteford, Kirkwood, East Lake and in the early years of the school, John B. Gordon.

In the summer of 1956, Julian called Sid Scarborough who held the position of Athletic Director for the City of Atlanta school system. Julian felt that he needed to make a change from Southwest due to some personality conflicts with the school's administration. But he also stressed that he only wanted to make a move if it included the varsity baseball team. Mr. Scarborough told him of a possible opening at Murphy and to stay in touch with him in case it materialized. Just a few days later, the opportunity did arise and Julian Mock accepted the job at Murphy. Along with his coaching duties, which included 8th grade basketball and B Team football as well as coaching varsity baseball, Julian taught 8th grade English and World History.

After he had gotten situated in his new school, he and Dot decided they would need to relocate to be closer to this school. They were still living in the southwest section of Atlanta and the commute was proving to be too much strain on them as a couple but, as Julian put it, "more strain on the old jalopy I was driving to and from school." They found a house on Crestmoor Drive in Decatur and settled in to their new life.

Murphy had a well-established athletic program in place and Coach Mock joined a group of good coaches. They included: Arthur Armstrong (Athletic Director and Varsity Football), Bennie Davis (Boys Basketball), A. T. Harmon (Girls Basketball), and Frank Irwin (Asst. Football).

The new coach would certainly have his work cut out for him. He was inheriting a baseball team that had gone 1-17 the previous year. He knew that if they were going to turn things around, the boys who would be playing on the 56-57 team would have to quickly buy into his philosophy. Coach Mock believed that there were two primary elements in being successful on a baseball diamond. He said, "First, you must work hard in practice. I believe in stressing the fundamentals of the game and even though they can sometimes be boring, they are essential to success. Laying down a perfect bunt can sometimes be just as critical as getting a base hit and hitting the cut-off man on a throw from the outfield just might stop a run from scoring. They're not as flashy as a big home run, but they are more important."

He was one of the first baseball coaches in the city, if not the first and only at that time, to build a sliding pit at the practice field. For those who are uninitiated as to what this is, it is a boxed-off area about ten feet long by five feet wide filled with sand or if good quality sand was not available- dirt. At the end of each practice, when the players were already dog-tired, the coach would line you up in a single file about twenty yards behind the pit and you would run full speed and when you got to the sand, you would slide as if you were going into second or third base. If you did not show the proper form and technique, you'd go to the end of the line and do it over again. Standing next to the pit, Coach Mock would shout out encouragement when you did it right or instruct you on what you were doing wrong, even showing you, personally, how to do it right when needed. As basic as this seemed, the discipline to do something as simple as slide properly, became the trademark for teams he coached.

Another practice ritual was infield practice. Anyone who has watched a baseball practice has seen a team go through this exercise. The coach hits a ground ball to the third baseman. He throws it to first who usually throws it to the catcher and the ball is thrown "around the horn." Then, the ball is hit to the shortstop and the routine begins again. The purpose of the drill is to develop good fielding and throwing skill, certainly, but if done seamlessly, it can have a huge affect on the opposition.

Floyd Harris, an excellent shortstop who played for Coach Mock in 1963 and 1964 once said: "I believe we won 90% of our games before the first pitch was ever thrown. The other team would watch us taking infield and you could literally see their jaws drop in amazement at how good we were. We were so flawless with our fielding and precision that you could imagine them saying to themselves, 'there's no way we can beat this team.' And most of the time, they were right."

"The second thing that is important," Coach Mock went on, "is hustle. You have to hustle every minute during a game. And hustle is not always physical. You have to hustle mentally as well. Know the situation. Know what you are going to do if the ball is hit to you. Know your opponents strengths and their weaknesses. If they have an outfielder, for example, who doesn't have a strong throwing arm, know when, as a runner, you can take an extra base. Know how to move a runner over even if it means sacrificing yourself."

But his players knew they had better physically hustle, too, meaning their heads needed to be in the game at all times. "If a player ever loafed on Coach Mock," Jimmy Battle, another former player said "they would catch an earful but even worse, they would get a wad of tobacco spit on their cleats. That caught your attention real fast."

There are several stories regarding incidents in games when hustle was the difference between winning and losing. One of the best occurred in 1959. It was a simple play- a play that could have been overlooked in the big scope of things, but it turned out that it helped Murphy win a game that they might not have without it.

With two outs in the inning, the Murphy batter had drawn a walk and the last pitch had gotten away from the catcher. Normally, the batter would simply trot down to first base but this was a Murphy player so he hustled down to first base. The catcher was loafing back to the backstop not concerned about anything more happening on the play. The batter, now the runner, noticed this lackluster effort and didn't stop running. He made it to second without a throw. The next Murphy batter singled and, because of his hustle, the runner scored easily. That turned out to be the winning run and it would not have happened without hustle. Those winning traits of a Murphy team started in 1957.

(Author's Note: During this next phase of Coach Mock's story, we will talk about the individual Murphy teams year-by-year. Some who played for him will be named, others won't. I hope that readers of this book who played for him but are not mentioned will forgive the omission. It is not meant as a slight to anyone; it is just that there is not enough time or space to do justice to all the fine athletes who played for him. What is more important to the story is the quality of the teams Julian Mock coached rather than individuals because all of us know that the most important thing to Julian Mock was TEAM.)

1957

After the dismal record of the 1956 team, no one knew what to expect from the squad that would take the field in 1957. There were several good players returning as well as some sophomores making the team for the first time. Among them: Paul Ard, Melvin Clay, Jimmy Gary, Robby Robinson, Johnny Guthrie, and the Gentle Giant, Morris Mitchell.

In an era where young teenage boys were not as big as they are now, Morris Mitchell literally stood head and shoulders above the rest. At 6'6" and weighing over 200 lbs., Mitchell was a redwood standing in a field of scrub pines. Because of his height, Mitchell was an imposing figure at the plate but even more critical to the team standing at first base. Larry Green, a fine-fielding third baseman who would play with Mitchell on the 1959 team said, "With Morris at first, you knew you didn't have to make a perfect throw every time. If your throw was a little high, Morris just had to lift his arm a few inches and he could catch it. He could make you look real good."

As might be expected, Mitchell was also an excellent basketball player. In 1958, he was a key figure in helping Murphy win the only boys basketball State Championship they would ever win.

Murphy played in the highest, at that time, classification in the state-AAA. They entered the State Tournament with a record of 24-4. The tournament was being held at Georgia Tech's Alexander Memorial Coliseum. Murphy cruised through the first three rounds defeating Savannah, Rossville, and Northside of Atlanta easily. The championship game was to be held on March 1, 1958 against city rival Brown High School.

The game was close and tense from start to finish. Tied at the end of regulation, the teams played to another tie at the end of the first overtime. The game went to a second and then to an unbelievable third overtime. Mitchell had been a standout in the post the entire game. Being as essential as he was to the scoring and defensive aspects of the game, Coach Bennie Davis had left him in the entire game. Morris Mitchell had played the entire 41 minutes of the game.

Watching at home was an eleven year-old boy by the name of Randy Blalock who worshipped Mitchell. The high school star lived near him and Randy would go to Morris' house often to shoot hoops with him. "Morris never treated me as a "little kid" or a "pest". He would spend hours with me teaching me shooting techniques and even though he wasn't the greatest ball handler in the world, big men weren't supposed to be, he taught me how to dribble. Whenever other guys came by and a pickup game would develop, Morris always picked me for his team. Being an only child, he became my adopted big brother."

The game was being broadcast locally and for those watching on TV or for those seeing it in person, the game was a classic. Randy remembers the game to this day. "Growing up across the street from the school, I would frequently attend the basketball games. I followed all of the players from that era but I always cheered extra hard for Morris."

"After the third overtime, it was decided that the next team to score would win the game and the State Championship. I don't know if this was the rule at the time or if the officials just made the decision at that moment, but that was the way it would end. Everything was riding on the tip off."

"Mitchell had a height advantage over his opponent but due to great timing, the other center had won the tip a few times. My heart was in my throat as the referee tossed the ball into the air. This time, however, Morris Mitchell was not going to be out-jumped. He soared in the air batting the ball to a streaking teammate who laid the ball in the basket for an easy score in a beautifully-designed play by Coach Davis. Murphy, and my hero, were State Champions winning 50-48."

Murphy made history that year when the girls' team also won the championship marking the first time in Georgia High School history that the same school had won both the boys and girls tourney in the same year.

Coach Mock also remembers Mitchell fondly. "He was one of the most easy-going, mild-mannered kids I've ever coached. I don't think I ever saw him lose his temper at himself or anyone else. And it's a good thing. With his size, he would have crushed somebody if had ever gotten really mad at them."

"In fact, the only time I ever heard him raise his voice at anyone was a day at practice when one of our players was giving the batter a lot of lip cause he kept fouling off pitches. The player in the field yelled at the batter, calling him some unkind names, and Morris finally had had enough. He took two steps toward the player, that's all it took, and told him in no uncertain terms to shut up. The player understood immediately that Morris was serious. He never said another word."

There was immediate improvement seen in 1957 as the team had a record of 8-6. This record, nor any of the other records shown in this section, include pre-season games, which Murphy usually won. Coach Mock did not keep track of those games. He only kept track of region and playoff games. Suffice it to say that his overall coaching record far surpasses what will be shown here.

Coach Mock has nicknames for several of the teams he coached at Murphy. He called this one "Transition Team" because they were moving from the old era to the new one. "They accepted me and my coaching style, which was certainly different and more demanding than the previous one, from the very first day. They weren't one of my better teams, but they worked as hard to get better as any of them. It was fun coaching back then because your players would listen to you without thinking they knew more than you. And, if necessary, you could discipline them without worrying about getting yelled at by their parents."

Prior to the baseball season, Coach Mock also found success on the hardwood. Mock led the B Team basketball team to an undefeated season. Many of those players had significant roles in helping Murphy win the State Championship that was detailed previously.

Julian Mock, only 28 years old himself, was not ready to hang up his own personal spikes just yet. He kept himself in good shape that summer by playing for an East Atlanta semi-pro team. He found himself back at his old second base position but one thing had not changed- he could still hit. He finished that season hitting over .400.

1958

The 58' team had many returning players from the previous year so, the outlook was good for an even better record than 57'. Along with Mitchell, Clay, Gary, and Guthrie from last year's team, new names such as Freddie Chandler, Jerry Hill, Gene Hudgins, and Tony Webb emerged. The team, however, would post a 9-7 record. Not exactly what the Atlanta sportswriters, who picked them to win the East Sub-Region, predicted.

"We just couldn't get consistent pitching that year." Mock would say. "As a matter of fact, inconsistency all the way around was our downfall. We'd tear the cover off the ball one game and only get two hits the next. Only one player, John Guthrie, played really well the entire year."

John Guthrie graduated in 1958 and he would go on to be one of the most noted graduates that Murphy ever produced. John Guthrie died in 2010 at the age of 70. *The Atlanta Journal* had this to say about him: *A former basketball coach at the University of Georgia from 1969-1978, John Guthrie's historical significance at the university may be more for the recruitment and signing of the school's first black basketball player. Guthrie, an Atlanta native who attended Murphy High School, was an assistant coach for the Bulldogs from 1969-1973, then spending five seasons as head coach. Before going to Georgia, Guthrie also coached at Southwest DeKalb and Oglethorpe. After his stint at Georgia, he served as a long-time assistant commissioner in the SEC, where he oversaw the league's basketball officials*

But the recruitment of Ronnie Hogue was not his only achievement in the field of race relations. As head of SEC referees, he made sure that the league was hiring qualified minorities. While at Georgia, he also brought on the first black assistant coach. One of his former players called him "a man far ahead of his time- a man I admire and think of as a father figure." Guthrie was an All-State basketball and baseball player at Murphy High School in Atlanta and graduated from Oglethorpe in 1962.

The future of baseball at Murphy also appeared brighter because of several up-and-coming players on the B Team. They finished their season undefeated in league play. The start of a dynasty was in the making.

Julian Mock could never quit coaching it seemed. Coaching multiple sports during the school year, he would also coach various American Legion teams or the Connie Mack League team at DeKalb Memorial during the summers. DeKalb Memorial was one of the premier Little League, Babe Ruth League, and Connie Mack League organizations in the city, if not the entire state. Most of the young lads who played for the Coach at Murphy continued honing their skills at DM. Blessed with a group of caring parents who worked as hard keeping the field and the concession stand in tip top shape as they did at their regular jobs, the organization was the gathering spot for everyone who lived in southeast Atlanta during the 50's and 60's.

Early in the year of 1958, Julian came home to the house in Decatur one night to the open arms of little two year-old Terry. She jumped up in his arms and told him, "Go have din-din." He sat down at the table and, this time, it did not take him long to figure out the meaning of the fourth place setting at the table. Without a word, he kissed Dot and Terry and with all the confidence in the world he told them, "This time it's going to be a boy." Alan Paul Mock was born on September 2, 1958. (seems to be a theme with these September births- you do the math)

1959

The male students who attended Murphy could be influenced by Julian Mock in two ways. Certainly, those who played for him, either on the basketball court or the baseball diamond, were affected by him. But others could get to know him through his classroom teaching, particularly, those who took Mechanical Drawing.

There were two elective courses that boys could select to go with their curriculum courses. Those two courses were Wood Shop or Mechanical Drawing. Julian was approached by the principal one day asking if he could teach the Mechanical Drawing class the following year. Never one to shy away from a challenge even though he had no idea what Mechanical Drawing was, much less how to teach it, Julian told him that he could.

He then sought out a friend who knew the subject well and at nights during that summer, he and the friend would get together and Julian "learned" the subject. He admits readily that those students that first year didn't get a quality class because he still didn't know what he was doing but, "I faked it well."

The young men of the B Team arrived the spring of 1959 ready to make the varsity and many of them did. Larry Greene, Jimmy Battle, Mike Fisher and Butch Jennings joined returners Webb, Hill, Clay, Bill Spencer, and Mitchell for his final year. A new transfer student named Bobby Dalgleish also helped make this team formidable.

But even with good teams there can sometimes be underlying factors that disrupt its potential. Such was the case with this team, but Coach Mock used that situation as a learning lesson for himself and became a better coach because of it.

"We finished the season with a 13-5 record but we could have been so much better. I only found out about the problem after the season and if I had known it existed during the season I could have reacted to it and, who knows, we might have won it all." Coach Mock reflected.

"There was some dissension for various reasons among several of the players. Jealousy of not getting enough playing time because they thought they were better than the kid playing, I don't know. But a few of the boys just didn't like each other. That can happen with any group of teenagers. I never saw it on the practice field but I did see some pouting and anger in the dugout. My problem was, I never addressed it or did anything about it. I take the blame. I guess they felt they couldn't come talk to me. I assumed, incorrectly, that I had an open door policy. By the time I knew it, our season was over. "

"I decided during that summer that I would never let that happen again. I would always have one player, a boy that I could trust and that was trusted by his teammates to be my eyes in the locker room- a pulse that can detect the attitude of the team. He wouldn't be a spy or a snitch, just my lookout for problems so that I could react to them before they festered into something bigger. "

1960

The school year for a coach during that era was a long succession of one sport after another. Coaches were required to coach multiple sports unlike today when they can specialize in their primary area of expertise. As soon as a coach arrived in the fall, football began. In Julian's case, as soon as football ended, basketball began. And when that season ended, baseball started. But what a start this would be. 1960 began a four-year stretch of championships at Murphy that ensured the legend and legacy of Coach Julian Mock.

B Team basketball, still coached by Julian, again got the attention of the school when they won the City Championship by defeating Brown. While a terrific accomplishment, it was nothing compared to what that year's baseball team would do.

The fourteen young men who made the cut during the rigorous tryouts were comprised of a few holdovers from the previous team, but many new faces surfaced as well. Those fourteen, as shown in the official team photo were: Danny Tate, Gil Shearer, Charles Burrows, Jimmy Battle, Mike Fisher, Bill Tyson, Larry Greene, Wayne McDaniel, Dan Spier, Roy Jarrett, Weldon Crook, Jere Ard, David Guthrie, and Jimmy Hobson.

Showing great promise in several warm-up games, mainly against schools from the West Sub-Region of Atlanta, Murphy headed into region play undefeated. During region play they only had one slipup in a game against North Fulton, taking a record of 13-1 into the City Championship series against Sylvan. The highlight of the region season was a no-hit game pitched by Weldon Crook against Grady and Coach Mock's longtime friend, Red Whitsett.

Murphy had a perfect combination of good pitching led by Crook (7-1, 1.73 ERA), Charles Burrows (3-1, 2.03 ERA), and newcomer David Guthrie, the younger brother of John Guthrie. Good pitching combined with good hitting is always a great combination and Murphy could hit. Not known for power, Murphy could "single and double you to death," as one opposing coach was quoted to say.

When not pitching, David Guthrie was a prolific hitter. He led the team in average (.343), runs batted in (24), and hits (23). And, by the way, he also finished the season with an 8-1 record and a 0.84 ERA. Larry Greene, who hit .303, led the team in runs scored with 25. Also contributing was Roy Jarrett (.298), Crook hit .294 when not pitching, and Gil Shearer.

Murphy was set to meet Sylvan for the City crown and for the first time, a game would be played at Murphy. Before 1960, Murphy's "home games" were played at Kirkwood Park but with the help of a group of parents and some City of Atlanta directed funds, a diamond was laid out next to the football practice field on the grounds of Murphy. Several fathers spent some long hours after work to build the dugout on the first base side of the diamond that would house future War Eagles.

The upkeep of the field and the baseball equipment issued under his responsibility were always extremely important to Julian. "That baseball field was his pride and joy." his daughter, Terry, related to me in an interview. "I was only five or six years old and I spent a lot of time at the field with him. Mom and I and later, Alan, my brother, watched just about every home game Murphy would play. We had an old VW bug back then and Dad had rigged up a contraption that he would hook to the rear bumper to drag the field. He would let me ride in the car with him which was a great thrill to me. We zoomed around the infield stirring up the dust behind us and then he "let me" hose down the infield. He always told me, 'If the boys are going to play well, they've got to have a good field to play on.' Anything he was involved with had to be done first-rate."

Ken Mozley, who played varsity baseball for Coach in 1964 remembers that during the early practices of the season before any actual games were played, the team had another major job to do before practice was considered over. "We would sometimes practice on Saturdays and Coach would always tell us to bring a sack lunch. But the sacks were used for more than just holding our sandwiches. After we had finished eating, we'd form a line on the first base side and walk across the diamond picking up rocks as we went. The primary reason for the sacks would be to serve as the place we stored the rocks as we picked them up.

"We also had to be very careful in taking care of the equipment, the bats and the balls, particularly." Randy Carroll added. "Woe be it to someone who broke a bat. It was like you were taking money out of coach's personal pocket." Randy added, "Before the fence was put up in the outfield at Murphy, well-hit balls would roll down the hill in the outfield down to a creek that ran between center and left field. Well, if we started with ten practice balls during batting practice, we darn well better have ten when we finished. The hill in center was covered in thick briars that would cut you to pieces so, a few of us got smart and hid some balls where we would know exactly where to find them. Then, if there was one ball that was in the middle of a briar thicket or one we just couldn't find at all, we'd go to our secret stash so we'd always be able to bring back as many as were lost."

The best two out of three series started out in Murphy's favor as they drubbed Sylvan 14-2 on the strength of a fine pitching performance by Weldon Crook. With Guthrie pitching the second game, things looked positive. But in his only loss of the season, Sylvan bested Guthrie, 5-2.

The biggest game of the season loomed ahead of them but confidence was high because everyone knew that Crook would be named the starter and after his performance in the first game, the outlook seemed positive. But in a surprise move, Coach Mock called on lefty Charles Burrows to start the game. Burrows was the third man in the rotation and had started only a few games, mostly appearing in late innings of blowout games.

Larry Greene remembers being "shocked." Wayne McDaniel, the catcher for the team, thought "Coach Mock had lost his mind." None of this was meant to undermine Burrows who everyone felt was a solid pitcher, "but when you had someone like Weldon Crook ready to go, you just naturally assumed he'd be your guy." Jimmy Battle remembers.

No one knows what is in the heart of a competitor, however. Burrows, a crafty pitcher who used breaking balls more so than speed, threw a 3-hit shutout and Murphy won the City Championship by a score of 5-0.

The state tournament was being held in Thomaston, Georgia, supposedly a neutral site situated in the middle of the state. The Georgia High School Athletic Association's AAA classification had four regions, two from the north and two from the southern portion of the state. Joining Murphy in the double-elimination tourney was Moultrie and Benedictine from the south and powerhouse Griffin High School.

Murphy got off to a good start by defeating Griffin 3-0 in the first round and Moultrie, 2-0 in the second. Griffin beat Benedictine in the second round eliminating them after they lost to Moultrie. Griffin then beat Moultrie, sending them home which set up another game with Griffin. If Murphy won, they'd be state champs. But as Coach Mock recalls, "the wheels fell off that day. We couldn't do anything right. We couldn't hit and we certainly couldn't pitch. We lost 18-2!" This set up a winner-take-all game. It turned out to be a classic.

David Guthrie started on the mound that day and Jimmy Fordham, Griffin's ace, was his opponent. Both pitchers were spectacular. Fordham gave up a few hits along the way as had Guthrie but no runs had crossed the plate through the regulation seven innings even though Griffin had come close loading the bases in the fourth with no outs. Coach Mock went out to the mound to make sure Guthrie was all right. "Let's see if we can figure out what to do, David." He calmly told him. Then he looked up at his pitcher who was several inches taller and said, "Oh, I know- strike em out!" Guthrie took the ball and proceeded to do just that, striking out the side with no runs being scored. "They never even fouled off a pitch." said Dan Spier, watching from the dugout.

Both pitchers were still throwing hard going into the eleventh. Still no runs: 0-0 after ten innings. Then, in the top of the 11th inning, Murphy's bats finally erupted. "We had hit shots right at them all day," Roy Jarrett recalls, "finally, they started falling." Murphy pushed across four runs and led 4-0 with Griffin coming to the plate.

The lead-off batter for Griffin got a single and Coach Mock thought that Guthrie had had enough. He brought in a fresh Weldon Crook who finished the game without any further damage and the Murphy High School War Eagles were the State Baseball Champions of Georgia.

Murphy averaged over seven runs a game while giving up an average of just over two runs. "And if you take out the game that Griffin beat us so badly, it was less than two runs a game."

Mock's nickname for this group was "The Competitors."

1961

The 1961 team was comprised of essentially the same fine players as the previous years' team so the prospects for a potential repeat championship were not out of the question. A few positional changes were made but the roster was the same.

The reasons for the position changes were due to another coaching discovery that Julian made which helped him the rest of his coaching career. As a coach, Mock usually subscribed to a personal rule that if you played a particular position for him one year, you would play the same position the next year. "Of all people, a guy who made a switch from second base to the outfield, I should have known that sometimes change is good."

So, when a disciplinary dismissal caused him to lose one of his outfielders, Coach Mock made a change. "The result probably was the reason the 61' team jelled and became state champs."

Again, the 61' team sailed through sub-region play showing only a tie against their old nemesis, North Fulton, as the only blemish on their record. Among the eleven victories were three shutouts and five games only giving up one run. Murphy outscored its sub-region opponents 100-18.

For the second straight year Murphy would be facing Sylvan for the city championship. The results of that epic series have been detailed previously in this story. "There has never been a better three-game series, no matter the level of competition, in the history of baseball." *The Atlanta Constitution* reported.

Heading into the state tournament, the Eagles were 15-1-1. When they left Thomaston, they were 15-3-1, losing both games they played. "Both games were close. We lost to Benedictine 3-0 and then Lanier knocked us out 5-3. A hit here or a strikeout there and things might have been different but the breaks didn't go our way." Coach Mock recalls. In typical great coach-speak he added, "That's not to take anything away from those two teams. They played well and deserved to win. It just wasn't in the cards for us that year."

It would be easy to focus on what this team didn't win but Coach Mock prefers to remember what they did win- the City of Atlanta Championship. He calls this team "The Hustlers" and for anyone that ever played for him, you know that is the best compliment he can give.

1962

With only a few exceptions, the 1962 squad was a rebuilding year. Joining returners Tate, McDaniel, Jarrett, Spier, Manning, and Frank Johnson were players who would become prominent in their own rights. Cleve Fowler, Jimmy "Rooster" Berry, Randy Carroll, Pete Alday, Jimmy Blissett, Mac Perry, Bob Maher, Max Ivey, Al Huff, and Dwight Langley made up the roster. And also joining them was a newcomer who would add his name to the list of quality pitchers Murphy historically produced- Tommy Yates.

High school baseball was not the end of the road for several of these athletes. Roy Jarrett, Cleve Fowler, and Randy Carroll would continue their baseball careers at Georgia Tech; Wayne McDaniel would play football at the University of Florida; and several others at smaller colleges. But the sky was the limit for Tommy Yates.

Along with being an excellent baseball player, Yates was a highly-sought football recruit. Long before what we now see in college football recruiting, Yates would have been considered a five-star prospect. An offensive guard and linebacker on defense, Yates played a major role in helping Murphy win many games, including the 1962 City Championship.

Yates would accept a football scholarship offer from Florida State but his career never developed to its full potential. But during his shining moments in high school, he was dominant when on the pitcher's mound.

Once again, for the third consecutive year, Murphy would win the City Championship, this time defeating West Fulton two games to none. Once again, they were in the Final Four playing for the State Championship.

Murphy would lose its opening game to Willingham placing them in the precarious position of having to play through the loser's bracket in the double-elimination tourney. But on the strength of a one-hit pitching performance by Cleve Fowler, the Eagles beat Richmond Academy.

The only team in the state that could rival Murphy for its baseball supremacy during these years was Griffin. As already noted, Murphy had faced them in the state finals the last two years, winning once and losing once. Griffin had not lost as yet in the tournament so a win over Murphy would give them the title again. Murphy prevailed, however, setting up yet another decisive game against them. Murphy jumped out to a 5-0 lead in the first inning but could not hold on as Griffin roared back to take the championship with a 10-5 win.

Fowler said of that game, "Us jumping out to such a big lead made the loss hurt even more. We didn't let up- Griffin was just that good. They could really hit. We were pretty tore up after that game but Coach Mock wouldn't let us stay down on ourselves. He'd tell us, 'get that dying-calf-in-a-hailstorm look off your face.' You had to smile after hearing that."

(Author's Note #2: One of the primary resource materials for this section of Julian's story have been the various annual yearbooks for Murphy, or *Azuwur,* as they were so cleverly called. The problem with using them is that they were generally a year behind in their discussion of the team. By the time the annual was being sent to press, the current year's team was in full swing so the results they reported were the previous year's results. I, once again, apologize if names of players for certain years don't exactly match up with the proper year. Coach Mock and I have done our best to be precise in the reporting but, after all, it has been over fifty years since these games happened.)

The 1962 *Azuwur* had the following: *Under the capable leadership of Coach Julian Mock, Murphy's baseball team has won the City Championship for the second consecutive year. [It would become four consecutive years] A team with such finesse and athletic ability is seldom found at the high school level. Murphy is justly proud of this outstanding team.* Truer words were never spoken.

1962 was "The Ambitious Team."

1963

In November of 1963, our country would experience one of the most devastating and traumatic events we had ever had as a nation. When the news came over the various media outlets that day that President John F. Kennedy had been shot and killed in Dallas, Texas, time came to an abrupt halt. For the students of Murphy High School in Atlanta, Georgia, it was no different.

During these moments when, as young students deeply affected by the death of this charismatic political leader, we needed someone to help us through these dark days, Coach Mock, the baseball coach, became Mr. Mock, the teacher. He was certainly not alone because the entire staff of Murphy pulled together to help us understand what had happened and what we needed to do to go on.

One of his students remembers that Julian simply asked his class to bow their heads and remain silent. This simple, yet powerful, act had a lasting impact.

But earlier that year, before the turmoil, life went on as usual and for fans of Murphy baseball, that meant another special season was on tap. In fact, this would be the season of "Perfection."

Coach Julian Mock had always been innovative in his coaching. As mentioned earlier, he was one of the first high school coaches to install a sliding pit but baseball was not the only area where he showed innovative skills. To help his basketball players improve their dribbling skills, he developed "blinders". These were glasses that the player would wear that prohibited them from looking down. The purpose was so that the player would keep his head up to see where they were going and not be dependent on looking down at the ball while dribbling. One of the drills that he instituted and was used by the varsity team as well was to dribble around several folding chairs switching from your left to right hands as you did so. After much practice the player could do this smoothly and seamlessly making it easier to handle the ball in heavy defensive traffic during games.

But he was also able to help individuals with their skills, both mentally and physically. Two of his former players related personal experiences that help illustrate that point.

Randy Carroll was a gifted natural athlete. He had played football for Murphy but was a star on the basketball and baseball team. Randy would go on to play baseball for Georgia Tech where he later served as their color analyst for the team's radio broadcasts for many years. He had been drafted by the Cleveland Indians but that didn't mean that he was perfect in every aspect of the game as he readily admitted.

"I had been a shortstop all my life. That was kind of a star position and I will admit that I was comfortable there so, when Coach Mock asked me to move to second base, I kind of balked at it in the beginning. But I soon realized that it was best for the team so I tried to learn the position as best I could."

"I was struggling with the transfer of the ball from the glove to my throwing hand, especially in trying to make the throw to the shortstop to begin a double play. Everything was backwards. At shortstop, you transfer your body from left to right; at second, it is the opposite. My glove transition was slow meaning my throw to the shortstop was not always on time."

"Coach Mock told me to stay one day after practice to take some extra fielding practice. As he approached me, I noticed that he was carrying a ping pong paddle and some tape. What in the world are those for, I thought. He told me to take off my glove. He taped the paddle to my left wrist and said, 'I'm gonna roll you some balls. I want you to field them with the paddle and flip them into your hand. This'll help you with your transfer.'"

"It took a while to get the hang of it but eventually I was able to make the flip. We must have spent an hour on that drill. I was exhausted but the balls kept coming. Finally, he said, 'OK, put your glove on.' Now, using the same technique, I could make the transfer, turn my body and have plenty of time to make an accurate, timely throw. I don't think there was another coach in the country that would have thought of that."

Coach Mock added, "Once Randy got rid of the over-sized fielder's glove he had been using and made the switch to an infielder's glove, well, that helped a lot, too."

And there were a few times that he had to use other methods to get the best out of his boys. Always quick with a jab or a comment, Coach Mock was never shy in doling out discipline when necessary. One of the best athletes to ever play at Murphy was Jimmy "Rooster" Berry. A three-star letterman, he let, by his own admission, his ego get in his way one day.

Berry, a third baseman, had developed a bad habit of turning his head slightly on sharply hit ground balls to him. To help him get past this flaw, Mock told him he was going to fungo ground balls to him. A fungo bat is a specially designed bat, generally longer and lighter than a regular bat, used by baseball coaches. Essentially, a coach skilled in the use of a fungo has better control and can direct the batted ball exactly where he wants it to go. Julian Mock was the "King of the Fungo."

Berry was instructed to field the ball and simply toss it to the side. The manager of the team would gather them as quickly as he could and return them to the bucket Coach Mock had at home plate. The stream of balls being hit at Berry seemed endless. Finally, an exhausted Berry remembers saying, "I've had it! I don't need this! I quit!" and he starts walking off the field.

Coach Mock says, "All right, quit! But you're going to have to make it to the bench first." As Berry took a few steps, the balls kept coming at him, only now they were being hit a little harder. The balls kept ricocheting off his body at an ever-increasing velocity until he finally gave up and went back to his position. The drill continued but it helped in making Jimmy Berry one of the best fielding third basemen in high school baseball that year.

And to get his point across regarding disciplinary matters, Coach Mock was never afraid to enforce his rules even to one of his better players. One year a star pitcher thought he could coast through Mock's Mechanical Drawing class. He was wrong. Coach Mock suspended him from the team until he brought his grade up. The player said later that it was one of the best things that had ever happened to him.

Carroll and Berry were just two of the reasons the 1963 team was so successful. Even when ranked with all of the other incredible teams Murphy had produced, this team stands above the rest. The reason Coach Mock called this team "Perfection" is because they were undefeated during the season and they remained undefeated throughout the playoffs.

The Murphy War Eagles of 1963 went 23-0. They won the City of Atlanta Championship for the fourth straight year and then proceeded to cruise through the State Tournament to win their second title in the past four years.

The team absolutely dominated their region opponents outscoring them 151-18, compiling a 14-0 record. Included in those fourteen games were six shutouts and two other one run games. Murphy scored double-digit runs in seven of those games. How's that for supremacy?

The format for the city tourney changed from its former best two of three matchup of the top team from each sub-region to a double-elimination format comprised of the top two teams from each sub-region. Murphy opened with a 5-3 win over West Fulton. Then, they drubbed Dykes 9-0 in the second round. Dykes and West Fulton then played an elimination game with West Fulton winning setting up a rematch of the first round. It was another tight contest but Murphy prevailed, 8-5 to win their fourth consecutive city championship.

Solid pitching and timely hitting was always Murphy's trademark but it was never as evident as during these games. Murphy won four straight: Westminster, 5-4; Jenkins, 14-0; Gordon, 3-2; and Lanier, 8-1. The highlight of the tournament, other than winning the championship, was the no-hitter Tommy Yates threw against Jenkins in the second game.

Once again, in the first game of the tournament, Coach Mock pulled one of his surprise pitching moves that had the entire team as well as the fans in the stands scratching their heads. For the regular season, the Coach had gone with a two-man rotation of pitchers Tommy Yates and Bud Moore with Cleve Rowley filling in here and there. The original plan had been to have another pitcher, Ronald "Butch" Crook, an excellent lefthander who later pitched for Georgia Tech, available but Crook had suffered a season ending injury before the season started. Realizing that he needed a little more depth, he called up sophomore Jimmy Beauford from the B Team. He then nominated Beauford, who had pitched effectively in the city tournament, to hurl the first game. Beauford didn't let him down. He needed Bud Moore to come in during the seventh to seal the victory but he pitched well enough to defeat Westminster, one of the better hitting teams in the state.

Murphy's starting lineup was consistent the entire year. Cleve Fowler, "My eyes and ears of the team. He was my coach on the field." Coach Mock said, was the catcher; Randy Carroll, 2nd; Jimmy Berry, 3rd; Jim Blissett played left field when Yates was not pitching, Roy Jarrett in center, and Mac Perry in right were the outfielders. Bob Morris, Bob Mahre, and Preston Loftin played valuable roles off the bench. And at first base and shortstop were two newcomers who had transferred to Murphy from Cleveland, Tennessee.

Twins Floyd (shortstop) and Lloyd (first base) Harris had enrolled at Murphy in 1962 and had made an immediate mark on its athletic programs. Along with baseball, they also starred on the basketball teams. Lloyd, who threw and hit left-handed, was a strong defensive player who had good power. Floyd, right-handed, was a human vacuum cleaner at shortstop. They, too, would join some of their teammates later at Georgia

Tech. In fact, at one time Georgia Tech had eight former Murphy players on its roster.

"We didn't have any stars, so to speak." Coach Mock would say. "We were just a team that relied on each other. We were always blessed with good pitching which in high school is so important but we could hit, too."

But a Murphy team was also always known for its execution and that was a direct reflection of the coaching they received from Julian Mock. As their record indicates, Murphy was blessed with good teams in its past but none was better than 1963.

1964

Graduation had a profound effect on the 64' team. Only the Harris twins, pitcher Bud Moore, Bob Morris, Preston Loftin, and a now-healthy Butch Crook were returning. But coming up from the B Team were some talented players: Juniors Ernie Green, Bobby Reynolds, Bill Crowley, Ken Mozley, and Dick Maher joined sophomores Jerry Owen and Jim Bello on the squad.

The team would achieve a record of 15-7 but would fall short of a fifth consecutive city title by losing to Southwest and Dykes in the playoffs. This elimination would also mean that Murphy would not have an appearance in the state tourney as well. The winning pitcher for Dykes that day was Billy Payne who would go on to have a successful football career at the University of Georgia as well as chairing the Atlanta Summer Games Olympic Committee which, as we all know now, were successful in obtaining the 1996 Summer games for Atlanta. Payne now serves as the Chairman of Augusta National Golf Course where we can see him each April awarding the coveted green jacket to the winner of the prestigious golf tournament, The Masters.

One of the highlights of the regular season that year occurred against Murphy's nearby rival, East Atlanta. Bud Moore is easily considered to be one of the best pitchers Murphy, a school always known for its quality pitching, ever produced. As mentioned previously, Moore would go on to have a stellar collegiate career at Georgia Tech. Murphy usually had its way with the Wildcats but on this day the teams were locked up in a great pitching duel with Moore on the mound for the Eagles. As he would be the first to admit, he was not the greatest hitter in the world. "But I really connected with a pitch late in the game and the wind must have gusted up cause it cleared the fence for a home run." Bud remembers. "That was the only run of the game and we won 1-0."

After experiencing the problems of personality clashes with one of his teams a few years before, Coach Mock always felt that the chemistry of a team was sometimes as important as the talent on the field. "I would frequently cut a better ballplayer over another during tryouts just because I thought the boy I kept on the team would fit better." Coach Mock would say. "This team had great chemistry. It's also good when one of the guys is so comical that the team just kinda revolves around him. We had that guy in our catcher, Ernie Green."

Coach Mock would go on, "Don't get me wrong, Ernie was a good catcher. He was solid behind the plate defensively but sometimes he was not real clear on the mental part of the game." Coach Mock recalled two episodes involving Ernie's lack of focus that made the team laugh.

Coach Mock usually called the pitches; fastball, curveball, etc., the pitcher was to throw from the dugout. The catcher, in this case Ernie, was to look to the dugout, get the signal from the coach, and relay it to the pitcher. Many times, Ernie had trouble remembering to get the signal which resulted in the pitcher, waiting to get the signal, and the catcher just staring at each other. And even when he did get the signal, he would often confuse them and relay the wrong signal. This was happening frequently during one game. Finally, the coach had had enough. Julian called time, went out to the pitcher's mound and told the pitcher, "Whatever signal Ernie gives you, throw the opposite. If he gives the signal for a fastball, throw the curve- if you see he wants a curveball, throw the bullet."

Ernie also had trouble remembering to wear some very vital protective equipment for practices. The team was taking batting practice one day and Ernie was behind the plate. A foul ball came straight back and caught Ernie in a place where no man nor boy ever wants to have a baseball hit. Writhing in pain at home plate, his teammates gathered around him, laughing at his discomfort. Julian calmly walked over to Ernie, bent down and said, "You weren't wearing your cup again, were you?" Since he couldn't speak Ernie just shook his head. Coach Mock then told him, "It's a damn shame that ball didn't hit you in the head instead of where it did because there ain't a doggone thing up there it could hurt."

Little did the team know as they came to the end of their season that the man who had been the coach of the Murphy baseball team for the last eight years would not be with them the following year.

Julian Mock's teams won two state championships, four City of Atlanta championships and played in five city tournaments and two other state tourneys finishing runner-up both those years. He was named the North Georgia All-Star Coach in 1959 and was the Coach of the Year for the state of Georgia in 1960 and 1963. He was Region Coach of the Year 1960-1963. And while no individual awards were given for B Team sports, his basketball teams won two city titles during his tenure at Murphy.

But when asked, one of Julian Mock's prouder accomplishments took place away from the diamond. In either 1961 or 1962 a group of influential baseball coaches in Atlanta high schools got together for the purpose of promoting and elevating high school baseball. Football and, to a little lesser degree, basketball, had always been at the forefront in the minds of the powers-that-be in Atlanta athletics. "Those two sports got the money, they got the resources, and they got the attention of the Board of Education. Baseball was always the wallflower at the dance." Coach Mock would say. "So, a group of us decided we needed to do something about it."

Julian Mock along with Red Whitsett (Grady), Bud Theodocian (Bass), Harry Lloyd (Westminster), and Jim Luck (Georgia Tech) formed the Atlanta Dugout Club. These men and all others who wished to attend would meet on a regular basis to discuss how high school baseball could be promoted better. Some of the positive decisions that came out of this club were the formation of 8th grade baseball throughout the city; a weekly Player and Coach of the Week Award helping to recognize the game more; and the institution of the Atlanta Dugout Classic, an annual tournament held at the beginning of the high school baseball season that kicked off that year's season. All of these innovations grew to the point that Atlanta high school baseball was held in the same lofty terms as the other sports.

The wheels were already in motion for a job move that would take Julian Mock away from the arena of athletics into the world of administration. But the legacy he had made at Murphy, not only as a coach, but as a teacher, a mentor, and a friend would remain in the thoughts and minds of all those he had touched for many, many years.

5th Inning

"Mr. Mock"

The winds of change swept through our nation and the city of Atlanta with ever-increasing velocity during the early 1960's. The country was seeing a marked political upheaval due mainly to our involvement in a war in Southeast Asia that few supported. A cultural revolution was going on around the youth of that era. After the death of JFK, our national leadership was in constant turmoil and many young people sought escape via the use of drugs. For the parents of these young people, it was a hope that we could return to the status quo.

The Civil Rights movement was in full swing and for four City of Atlanta high schools, Murphy being one of them, change came in the form of desegregation. Paranoia set in for many families causing an epidemic known as "White Flight" to run rampant. This movement to the suburbs by families who had been established in southeast Atlanta for decades resulted in a dynamic difference in the demographics of Murphy.

For one man, the change that was going on around him would cause him to look at his career and make the toughest decision he had ever had to make in his life. Coach Julian Mock was going to leave Murphy and his coaching life to become Mr. Mock, a school administrator.

Julian had been approached previously about this possibility but turned the opportunity down to remain at Murphy. Realizing, however, that he needed to be prepared for the eventuality of a career move, he had gone back to take the necessary classes to obtain his administrative qualifications. He obtained his Masters in Physical Education in 1956 and had begun his study for his Masters in School Administration which he would eventually complete in 1972. Now, in 1964, it was time for him to make the move that would also provide a higher income in order to better provide for his family.

When the thought of making a career move first entered his mind, he tried to find another coaching job outside Atlanta. But finding the proper fit with a school that needed both a coach and a certified Social Studies teacher proved to be difficult. The prospect of leaving Murphy loomed large as he faced the end of the 1964 school year. In his heart, he realized that, in all likelihood, he would not be coming back. He felt he needed to prepare a few of the students who would be returning for their Senior year, a year without Julian Mock, to that possibility so, he decided he would confide in a select few. One of those was Alice Arnold (Bowlden).

True to his use of nicknames, he always referred to Alice as A2, or A Square. Julian had served as her Home Room Teacher but, more significantly, she was his teacher's aide for his Mechanical Drawing Class. Alice was one of the most popular and sweetest girls to ever walk the halls of Murphy so it is not difficult to understand why Julian was so fond of her.

Alice remembers: "A few of us girls, certainly me, were jealous of the boys because they were able to be around him more than us. I just liked him from the start and I believe he liked me for some reason. We just 'clicked' and that was a blessing for me."

"Often, if he was going to be a little late for class, he would let me start the class by providing me with some notes on what we were supposed to cover. After a few minutes, some of the boys would nod off and lay their heads down on the drawing board desks where they sat. More than once did he tip toe in and use his famous T-square to bring them back to reality by rapping it on the side of their desk. In startled fright, their heads would bounce off the desk and I must admit that I got a few laughs when I saw the looks on their faces."

"When time would permit between classes, we would talk about his scouting for the Pittsburgh Pirates that he did during the summers. I still have one of his business cards from the Pirate organization. We talked about some of his past players, never his current ones, though. You could tell the ones that were his favorites as he talked about their commitment as well as their talent. I'm sure he was the same way as a coach because I definitely saw it in him as a teacher, he didn't put up with any nonsense. I learned many life lessons from him."

"He sat me down one day after class and told me that he was thinking about leaving. Naturally, I was heartbroken. I have no idea what I said to him- probably a lot of teary-eyed babble, but I knew our school would not be the same. Sure enough, when we came back in the Fall, he was no longer there."

"Most of his accolades came from being such a good coach but he was equally a good man. I guess I had a young girl crush on him and after being able to spend a good bit of time with him at our recent 50th Reunion, my husband says I still do."

Julian entered that summer doing the same thing he had done every summer for many years. He travelled around the South, mainly in Alabama, scouting for the Pirates and holding the baseball clinics he had become widely known for.

Daughter #1, Terry, remembers those summer scouting trips well. "Daddy was always a very frugal man- some might even call him cheap, so to reduce expenses as much as possible we always travelled around in that VW because it got good gas mileage. Later, the "Brown Bus" came along but in the early years it was just that VW."

"Long before the days of seat belts or car seats, my brother and I would be scrunched into that tiny back seat. You can imagine how that went with a little girl and a toddler trying to get along. The car had no air conditioner and there was a hole in the floorboard of the back seat with only a piece of metal covering it. Alan and I would slide the metal back and watch the road go by underneath us."

"Our luggage consisted of paper bags from the grocery and a Styrofoam cooler for Alan's bottles. One of my jobs was to look out for the cheapest motels, usually a Howard Johnson, when it came time for us to find a place to stay for the night. We pretty much existed on $.10

hamburgers during those days on the road which meant we ate a lot of Krystal's. I ate so many then, I won't touch one today."

"And the mornings were always fun because Dad would threaten to sing if we didn't immediately get up when he called us. Dad is a horrible singer, can't carry a tune for the life of him so, if we were too slow he'd start belting out *Oh What a Beautiful Morning!* That was all it took. We were up in a flash."

Terry also remembers that his frugality carried over to other areas, too. "We had some old furniture, a table and some chairs as I recall, that needed refinishing. They were scratched up pretty badly. Instead of taking them to a professional, he took them to school and had the Wood Shop class do the work as a class project."

During the summer of 64', Julian got another call from a Clayton County official asking him to consider an Assistant Principal position at the high school with a promise that he would be named Principal at a new Junior High that was under construction and scheduled to open the following year.

Julian went for an interview in July, still unsure of what he was going to do. But during the last week of July he went to Albany, Georgia to cover an American Legion tournament where he made up his mind. He accepted the offer.

For the first year or so of his employment in Clayton County, Julian would make the long commute from their Decatur home on Crestmoor to the school. The Interstate system was not fully complete at that time so the long drive made for very long days. And even though the two children at that time, Terry and Alan, were firmly entrenched at Wadsworth Elementary, Julian and Dot knew they would need to sell the house and move to College Park.

The move occurred in late 1965. The children, now 10 and 7, said goodbye to their friends but quickly settled into their new school. Terry recalls that the school they attended sat on what is now one of the runways at the airport. "We could look out the classroom window and watch the planes take off and land."

But for Julian Mock, one of the other important decisions was which church they were going to attend. Julian's faith was strong and extremely important to him as has been documented previously. He grew up going to church as a child and had been a steady church attendee ever since. While living in Decatur, the family had been members of Woodlawn Baptist. As a young man, Julian taught a Sunday School class comprised of, primarily, retired men. "I must not have been a very good teacher, though. They kept nodding off and falling to sleep while I taught. I always made it a practice to slam my Bible good and hard at the end of the class to wake them up."

In College Park, they joined 2nd Baptist Church where they regularly attended until they moved to Alabama. Julian is proud of his service to the church listing these positions of honor that he held while a member: became an ordained Deacon in 1971, Chairman of Deacons, Chairman of Finance Committee, and Chairman of Personnel Committee.

But one of his proudest accomplishments, along with accepting Christ in 1943, is the decision he and Dot made in 1958 to begin tithing. "You have to understand that we weren't making a lot of money then. We were raising two children, had a mortgage and all the other household expenses a young married couple incur, but we felt this was something we just had to do." He adds, "I am glad I can call myself a Christian. I was never one to throw my faith in your face, but if you ask me, I'll tell you that I am a believer and that I am saved."

The first year passed by quickly. As Assistant Principal, one of his primary duties, it seems from the comments received regarding this period in his life, was to dispense discipline when necessary. Paddling in Atlanta City Schools had been abolished several years prior but in Clayton County, it was still allowed. If a male student got the dreaded message, "Report to Mr. Mock's office", he knew that he might as well prepare for the eventuality of a paddling.

One of his teachers remembers that the paddle had holes in it, kind of like Swiss cheese, that could really wreak havoc on the backside. They said that Julian would really put his weight behind the swings and sometimes lift the boy off the floor. But he also added that there were very few repeat offenders. They got the message real quick.

Julian recalls one young man who, apparently, didn't get the message as quickly as others. The student was a constant repeat offender and Julian remembers that he was a smallish kid. "I never paddled more than three times, but this boy was so small the paddle would knock him to his knees each time. It almost became a laughing matter." Theses paddling sessions became so regular that Principal Mock finally told the boy, "Why don't you come by first thing every morning before classes start and get a good paddling. It'll last you for the day." Thinking him to be serious, the boy finally got the message and was never back in Julian's office again for disciplinary reasons. The boy went on to become an Honor student.

Julian's career took a different path for the 1965-1966 school year- a path slightly different from the one that had been originally proposed but a path that he would stay on for the next fifteen years. Unexpectedly, the previous principal resigned and instead of being named the principal at the Junior High, Julian was named Principal of North Clayton High School.

Never one to shy away from challenges, Julian met the ones presented by this new assignment head on. He explained the challenges like this: "I took over a school that was quite a bit different from Murphy. It was smaller in both the physical building aspect and student population. NCHS had a total of about 500 students in grades 8-12. The area itself was what could only be considered as rural. There was very little commercial or residential development seen in those years. There was much more farming done here than I expected."

"I inherited a school that was deeply in debt overall, but particularly the athletic department, which owed a large sum to a major Atlanta sporting goods store, with no real funding available and no way to raise income. We didn't even have a baseball team which, naturally, broke my heart. All we had was a football team, boys and girls basketball, and a track team with no uniforms. We had no girls PE coaches."

"My first year as Asst. Principal, I didn't even have an office. The building was falling down around us. Some days we didn't have heat. I know this sounds like the old I walked ten miles to school, uphill both ways, but it was some pretty bad conditions we were trying to work under."

But over the years two things changed which helped convert what, in his words, had been a rural school into a modern one. A new building was constructed and the old high school was changed to a Junior High. And the Atlanta Airport expansion brought in a new wave of people- higher income people like pilots and controllers who would be paying higher taxes.

One of the first things Julian did was to put in a baseball program. Enter Bill Kennedy. In order to start a baseball program, you needed a coach and in a circle of life-type twist, Kennedy was hired for that job.

Bill Kennedy grew up in the heart of Atlanta attending Grady High School, playing for Julian's long-time friend, Red Whitsett. Bill remembers facing a Coach Mock-led team on many occasions, "Usually on the losing side." he would add.

After graduating from high school, Kennedy attended the University of Tennessee. Looking for a coaching position, Bill called his old coach. Just like Whitsett had done years before helping Julian find his first job at Southwest, he told Kennedy that he knew someone who was starting up a baseball program and was looking for a coach. "I had no idea where Clayton County was but I gave Julian a call and he hired me."

He continued, "You always have a special place in your heart for the person who gives you your first job and that is certainly the case with Julian. But it goes much deeper than that. From day one he became my mentor. I would have been a fool if I had not listened to the advice of one of the best baseball coaches in the state. We would sit in his office every day after classes before the season was to begin and I would pick his brain. He taught me how to organize practices; how the baseball field should be laid out; what drills to run; and, yes, how to wear the uniform."

This was always an important aspect of the game to Julian. Each year, while at Murphy, the first day of practice would be devoted to how to properly put on and wear your uniform. This was not something he took lightly. He would show the team in great detail everything from how to lace your cleats to how to wear your cap. And the other cardinal rule was that you never jogged to your position, you sprinted.

"He'd help me out during practices but when it came time for the game, he never interfered. I was lucky enough to be his son's coach and that was a real honor but, again, he never forced me to handle Alan any differently than any other player. Truth is, I think he wanted me to be harder on him so no one could say I showed him any partiality."

When asked about Julian's administrative abilities, Kennedy would say: "He was tough- but fair. You knew exactly where you stood with Julian. He was quick to praise but quick to reprimand, when needed. We had a great relationship and he is, without question, one of the biggest influences in my life."

Kennedy was later involved in another ironic twist with Julian. When Julian decided to leave the Pirate organization to become a full-time scout with the Cincinnati Reds, he recommended Bill Kennedy to take over his area. Bill Kennedy scouted for the Pittsburgh Pirates until his retirement.

It was now 1970 and life at North Clayton had settled in to a regular routine during the school year. It had been one of those routine weeks, a week filled with reports and minutia, but now, as he drove home, he looked forward to a fairly activity-free weekend. The Valentine's Dance was behind him and the high school basketball team had a rare weekend off with no games scheduled. Other than church on Sunday and taking Terry, who was now 15, out for a driving lesson, he had nothing to do.

Yet, something was tugging at his brain. He had a "feeling" that something big was about to happen in his life but he couldn't put his finger on what it might be or how it might affect him. He got these sensations all the time. He'd had them all his life, in fact. He had them when it came to making baseball decisions like who to pitch, when to hit and run, and when to steal and the feelings had rarely let him down. He had them when it came to making financial decisions for the family. That usually meant turning the decision over to Dot, who was much better with money decisions than him. And he usually trusted his feelings with decisions at school. But he couldn't pinpoint this feeling at all.

Alan, now 12, bombed him with questions as soon as he opened the door. "Wanna go shoot some hoops, Dad? Did you know I got an A on my math test? Can we go see that new movie about the Korean War? I think its called Smash, or somethin' like that."

Dot interrupted the excited young boy, "Honey, let your Daddy get settled down. He's just barely gotten home from school and you're pounding him with questions. Let the man breathe. Go play in your room until after he's had his dinner then, maybe, he can give you some time."

Alan ran off to his room, shouting as he left, "Sorry, Dad. Just glad to have you home!"

Julian sat down in his favorite chair as Dot said, "Don't get too relaxed. I've got something I want to show you. I'll go warm up some soup for you. I'll call you in a couple of minutes."

It didn't take long for him to relax. His eyes got heavy as he was just about to doze off when he heard Dot call his name. As soon as his head cleared, the "feeling" came back. But as soon as he saw the table, he knew what the "feeling" was.

He looked at the table and there were now five place settings laid out on the table. It had taken a few years but the December free time a teacher has had worked again. The happy couple smiled at each other and Dot filled in the blanks. "I'm due in September again. Can you believe it? We're going to have another baby. Think we're too old (Julian would be 41 in May)?" Julian just shook his head and thought to himself, "So that's what that feeling was."

Christy Lynn Mock was born on September 28, 1970.

The adjustment from being a teacher to a coach was never an easy one for Julian. One of the biggest differences was that he was separated from direct contact with the students by a couple of levels. At Murphy, he had direct communication with them as their teacher or coach. At NCHS, he usually didn't get involved with them unless there was a serious problem. The direct contact was handled by the teacher or the

Assistant Principal. He missed interacting with "my boys and my girls", he would say.

Another of his staff members as well as being one of the coaches who confirmed that Julian missed the interaction with the students was Bob White. White, another graduate of the Atlanta School System (Fulton-1964), was hired by Julian in 1969 out of West Georgia. Like most people who meet Julian, White has a very high regard for him. "You always hold dear those that are meaningful in your life and the person who gives you your first job out of college is usually one of those people. That is certainly the case for me with Julian Mock."

"I had just graduated from West Georgia. I'll never forget that interview. Julian was firing questions at me and towards the end of the interview he admitted that he was really looking for someone with a little coaching experience rather than someone fresh out of school. I guess I was a brash kid who didn't know better but I spoke up and told him that nobody comes out of college with experience. The only way you can get experience is for someone to take a chance on you. Then I told him that what I lacked in experience I would make up in work effort. You'll never have anybody work harder than me, I told him. He told me later when he offered me the job that what sold him was even though I didn't have the experience he was looking for, my positive attitude convinced him I was the right guy for the job."

White, who still has a close relationship with Julian and Dot today, remembers that Julian ran a tight ship and that there was never any doubt in anyone's mind as to who was in charge. He admitted that many of the teachers called Julian "Little Napoleon". But never to his face, though.

"My first year, Julian wanted all of us who were to be rookie teachers to attend a walkthrough of a new JC Penney's Outlet warehouse that had just been built in our area. The excursion was set before school had started so the football coach decided to call a practice for that day. I was going to be an assistant coach so I was torn as to what to do- go on the field trip or go to football practice. I decided to go to the football practice. Big mistake! As the bus pulled out, I could see Julian glaring at all of the coaches. Great, I thought to myself. I've only been here one week and I'm gonna get fired."

"Nothing was said that day but the following day, the entire coaching staff was called into his office, even the head coach. He read us the riot act and in no uncertain terms told us that if anything like that (calling a practice on a day he had scheduled an event for the teachers) ever happened again, heads would roll."

It was years later that White discovered one of the other reasons why Julian had been so upset. Penney's had supplied food for those who were taking the excursion. They had sent over several sandwich trays and the fixins' to go with it. When the group got back to the school, there was hardly anything left- the coaches had eaten it all. Not only had his orders been disobeyed, he had to go without lunch that day.

White also recalls that Julian's faculty meetings were well organized. "He didn't believe in a lot of wasted time or motion." This characteristic is easy to understand for those who played baseball or basketball for him. Practices were always run efficiently with very little down time at all.

White shared lunch room duty with Julian and, even there, lessons could be learned. We always stood in the same spot every day- a spot where we had the best vantage point for seeing students who might be acting up. "He always said 'position is the key'. Actually, there was another reason he chose that particular spot. It gave us the best view of where the female teachers sat to have their lunch. I'd tease him and say that Miss Dot would kill him for looking at other women. He'd laugh and say, 'She knows I'm harmless besides just because I'm on a diet that doesn't mean I can't look at the menu.'"

In 1975, another aspect of Julian's life began with the start of his summer baseball clinics. He missed the direct contact of coaching so much that he thought this would be a great way to get back into coaching, if only during the summer months. John Guthrie, one of his former Murphy players and Harry Lloyd, the head baseball coach at Westminster who, along with Julian, had been instrumental in starting up the Atlanta Dugout Club, began the camps.

Harry Lloyd explained how these clinics were originally set up. "To begin with, we only invited boys from the ages of 13-17. This would eventually expand to include boys and girls of all ages, but in the beginning stages, we wanted to work with older high school age boys."

"For the first two or three years we held the clinics at Woodward Academy from Monday thru Friday for two weeks at a time. If schedules permitted, we might do two or three clinics a summer. We later moved to Berry College in Rome and then to Young Harris. We began getting a larger group for the clinics because we could offer overnight dormitory facilities where the boys could stay all week."

"We'd work on basic fundamentals. Admittedly, we began these clinics with the idea of working with youngsters who were already pretty good ballplayers who just wanted to improve their existing skills. After a few years, however, we started getting kids who had never played the game before. In a lot of those cases, we were nothing more than a babysitting service so we started screening the non-serious kids out. Really, we were screening their parents' out." The summer clinics continued in different locations and in different modes for some 35 years.

"I got to watch Julian coach these youngsters on a daily basis and while I thought I was a good coach, I would just stand back in awe of his knowledge of the game. I have been around and seen a lot of coaches/managers in my life and I can honestly say that I have never seen a better baseball coach in my life than Julian Mock."

Despite the hardships Julian had to endure during the first few years of his tenure at North Clayton, progress was made. "I admit that the change from coaching to being a principal was difficult at first. I eventually realized that I could help more people as an administrator than I could as a coach. As a coach, you can only help those that are on the team at that given time. As a principal, I could help the entire student body and by helping them I could also help their families."

Julian cites four programs that he instituted at North Clayton as being, in his opinion, the most significant changes he made while principal. "There were a lot of things we did at North Clayton that I am proud of, but these were the things I remember making the biggest changes in the attitude of the students and the faculty."

The first was a change in the daily lunch menus offered to the students. Julian has very fond memories of the dietician, Dorothy Simmons, who helped him implement these changes. "When we met to discuss these changes, she was excited about them from the start. Even though this would mean a little extra work for her staff and, certainly, for her, she bought into them immediately. She had children of her own, as did all of her workers, but she told me that she had often thought about doing something like this but previous administrators would never listen."

In the 1970's, under the Federal Lunch Program requirements, a school had to meet certain guidelines and budgetary constraints in providing what it deemed to be a nutritious lunch program each day. But it did not stipulate what you could serve the students each day. Julian's plan was simple- give options. Prior to this, as all of us who went to school prior to the 70's will remember, a student had two options. Bring your own lunch to school or buy the hot meal provided each day. North Clayton became the first school in the state to allow the student choices. A soup and sandwich combination, a slice of pizza, and a salad bar were just a few of the choices a student could choose from on any given school day. Student attitudes improved greatly and the cafeteria staff's morale improved as well.

Another problem affecting, not only North Clayton, but every other high school in the state, was the ever-increasing drop-out rate that was going on. There were many factors contributing to the growing number of students leaving school. Julian recognized that he needed to do something to identify these reasons and to take actions that would help to stem the tide of these numbers, keeping students in school.

His plan was to recognize the fact that not all students were college material. The War in Viet Nam was escalating so male students were leaving to join the service or going into the work force to begin making some money for no more reason than they wanted to buy a car. Girls, too, wanted jobs but with no skills and with no diploma, this was very difficult. Julian's plan was to designate four classifications of students and streamline their classes to fit their needs. The four classifications were: General- those that just wanted a high school diploma; College-bound; Business Education; and, Technical skills.

For the General Students, he began a "0" period class beginning at 7: 30 am. This would allow the student to leave school at noon each day so that they could go to jobs they might have. They would still be attending classes that would provide them with the necessary requirements for procurement of a diploma, but they could still find jobs to begin earning incomes. Even these classes were structured for the slow, medium, or fast-learning student. Faculty liked this as well because now their classes were not mixed giving them a chance to design their class plans accordingly.

College-bound students were identified and their class schedules were set up to provide them with the necessary tools to enable them to further their education. Even these classes were set up on either a medium or fast-paced basis.

A broader base of Business Education classes including typing, shorthand, and bookkeeping were developed. These were established to assist both male and female students who wanted to enter the business world but weren't interested in management jobs that required a college degree.

And, finally, a much broader scope of technical school classes were formed. For boys, shop classes like metal shop, woodworking, auto shop, and print shop were available while girls could choose sewing, homemaking, and even beautician classes. This wide variety of classes aimed, at identifying a student's career path, became very popular with the students and a marked improvement of North Clayton's drop-out rate was seen almost immediately.

The third achievement was a change in the way Phys Ed was handled at the school. As was mentioned previously, when he took over the school, there were no female Phys Ed teachers. That was remedied in his second year by hiring two teachers. "But the major thing we did," he said, "was to change the format of the classes. We made them low-impact and included what we called 'life time sports training'. We went away from the traditional dodge ball, rope climbing, volleyball activities to sports the kids could play their entire lives. Sports like golf, bowling, and tennis. This made Phys Ed more fun and when it is more fun, the students will participate better."

The final change Julian made was more for the faculty than the students but because it affected and improved the attitudes of the teachers, it trickled down to the students. Never being one who enjoyed meetings himself, Julian went away from the routine full faculty meetings that had been held before on a weekly basis. He would meet with the department heads on a monthly basis and they would make their reports to him. It would, therefore, be up to them to meet with the other teachers in their areas. This method gave the department heads more responsibility and authority, which they enjoyed and it was definitely a time-saving factor sinc the staff was not constantly in meetings. Fewer meetings for him also freed up time for him that allowed him time to focus on other issues.

Several of these programs became model changes that administrators from all over the state began adopting. It was not too long that the name of Julian Mock, school principal became as widely known as Julian Mock, baseball coach in Georgia education circles.

But any good administrator has to be adaptable and adjust their thinking over time. Julian admits that when he began this phase of his life, he had more of a czarist attitude than he should have. It was "his way or the highway" and he found out quickly that this style would not work as principal.

Julian was challenged with a tough disciplinary decision regarding one of the star players on the football team. When he made his decision, which was suspension for a big game, an unknown party took exception with the verdict by deflating the tires on his car one day. He decided that, perhaps, his punishment was a bit too strict and softened his stance going forward. The lesson he learned was that you could not be a dictator.

When asked about his philosophy of how to be a good administrator, Julian shares these words of wisdom. "I have often referred to the years I was principal as the Age of Dissent. This was the 70's and our nation was fighting against everything. There was a general disrespect for authority. To combat this with respect to how I ran North Clayton, I came up with my Four Principles off Being a Principal. The principles actually break down to four questions I needed to ask myself each time a crisis occurred."

> What? – Identify the problem. You can't solve a problem until you know what the problem is.
> How? – How am I going to lead my group as Principal to solve the problem.
> Where? – What resources, materials, or outside assistance do I need to find to help me lead.
> When? – Set timelines and deadlines on myself to solve the problem so that it doesn't linger and become an even larger problem.

"And I realized quickly that there was actually a fifth question. But if you wanted to be a good leader, you must force yourself never to ask it- Why? Never ask why you led or made the decision you made. Never doubt yourself. Trust your instincts and move forward."

This is a philosophy and a set of principles that he would definitely carry forward into the next phase of his life. After twenty plus years in the business of education, Julian Mock was ready to enter, yet another, career- a career that would take him back into the world of baseball.

6th Inning

"The Scouting Years"

The three tired travelers on that dark Alabama road were anxious to get to their destination. It had been a long day for all three but, especially tiresome for the young girl who slept in the backseat of the car. Just ahead were some travelling companions who were leading the way to the next small town where they might find a good place to stay for the night.

It had been a productive day for the man sitting behind the wheel. He had discovered some potential new talent and as the miles swept by, he talked quietly to the woman sitting in the passenger seat. After all these years of being with the man, she, too, had developed a keen eye for what he looked for and she shared her thoughts with him.

The man looked in the rear view mirror as he drove and noticed bright lights approaching at a rapid rate. The vehicle now loomed menacingly behind with their high beams shining brightly into their car. The man was going the speed limit, but he sped up slightly to see if he could put some separation between the two vehicles. With every mph he increased, the pickup truck behind him accelerated with him. Now, the truck was so close that he actually made contact with the bumper of the man's car.

The man looked for a place where he might pull over to let the truck pass, but there was no opportunity to do so. Besides, the man thought, if I slow down the driver may ram us and run us off the road. What did these guys want? Did they mean to rob us or were they just good ole boys who had had too much beer and were just out for mischief? There was no way to know. But above all, he had to think of the safety of the little girl in the back seat.

The man could tell that there were three men in the truck so a confrontation was out of the question. He blew his horn to get the attention of his friend up ahead but received no acknowledgement from him. Once again, the car was jolted as the truck pushed the rear of their car. The little girl began to stir so the man knew he had to do something fast.

Finally, he got a signal from the car ahead that they recognized the peril the man and his family were in. There were no oncoming cars, so the car ahead pulled over to the other lane so that the truck could see them. From both sides of the car, baseball bats appeared. The driver and the passenger waved the bats defiantly at the occupants of the truck who quickly got the message. They continued their chase for another half mile or so, but finally gave up. The truck slowed, pulled off the road, and turned around. The man breathed a sigh of relief, threw his hand up to thank the driver ahead, and continued their journey until they eventually found a motel.

Such was the life of Julian and Dorothy Mock during those scouting years of the 80's. Many long days were spent that were then culminated in long hours on the road; travelling from city to city looking for the next baseball superstar. Julian estimated that he travelled over forty thousand miles watching over three hundred games each summer during those years. And while this may have been the scariest episode he ever faced on the road, it was not the only adventure he and his family shared. But he wouldn't have wanted it any other way.

Julian Mock was never far away from the game of baseball. Even after he left coaching to become North Clayton's principal, he kept his hand, his head, and his heart in the game by scouting for Major League clubs. And in 1980, he launched his third career- this time as a full-time baseball scout. But let's go back a few years to see how this phase of his life got its start.

In 1959, after a very successful season at Murphy, Coach Julian Mock was selected to be the All-Star Coach for the North Georgia squad for its annual game against the South All-Stars. In essence, this was an honor signifying that he was Coach of the Year in North Georgia. The opposing coach was Lem Clark.

Later that summer, Coach Mock took an American Legion team he was coaching to a tournament. There in the stands taking notes was Coach Clark. Julian approached him and asked him what he was doing. Clark told him that he was a part-time scout for the Pittsburgh Pirates organization and he was there to scout a few players who were playing in the tournament. Julian asked him how he had gotten started with scouting and Clark related the story to him. He then asked Julian, "Would you like to do this?" The vigorous, "You bet I would" followed.

Clark went on to tell him that the Pirates had authorized him to find someone else to assist him in his territory and if Julian was serious, then he would give him some names of boys he wanted to scout but didn't have time to go see personally. "Understand, though," Clark added, "that you don't get paid unless we sign the kid and then you and I do a split. In other words, there's not a lot of money in it." That was okay with Julian. Anything to get his foot in the door. Anything to get to see more games during the summer.

From 1959 to 1968, Julian represented the Pirates as a Recommending Scout. Shortly after starting with them in 1959 it was recognized that he had a keen eye for talent so, he was given his own territory. It was during one of those trips that Julian remembers the funniest thing he has ever seen on a baseball field.

The event occurred in a small Mississippi town between two rival towns where the passion for baseball was intense. The bases were loaded for one of the teams and the player at bat laced a single over the second baseman's head. The first run scored easily but the right fielder made a strong throw to the plate to try and nab the sliding runner. The catcher swiped at the runner but missed the tag. That's when the fun started.

The catcher jumped up and told the umpire that the runner had missed home plate. "Then you need to go tag him before I can make a call." said the umpire. "Which one was he?" asked the catcher. "I don't know!" exclaimed the ump. "They're not wearing numbers. You'll have to tag everbody."

The catcher ran to the dugout which had openings on either end and entered the opening nearest home plate. He proceeded to go down the line tagging each ball player, looking back at the umpire each time for a call. None came so he kept going up the line tagging players as he went. Meanwhile, at the far end of the dugout, the true runner realized what was happening and he raced out of the entrance at the far end of the dugout in an attempt to go back and touch home plate. The catcher saw this and attempted to get out of the dugout and chase him down but was conveniently held up by some of the players.

He finally made it out, ball in hand, to see the runner about ten feet away from home plate. He knew he couldn't outrun him, but the pitcher had seen what was going on and had come to home to cover. The catcher threw to the pitcher and, in Mock's words, "the craziest rundown in the history of baseball began- a rundown, not on the base paths, but between a dugout and home plate. By the time the play was over, the first baseman, the third baseman, and the shortstop had gotten involved. To confuse matters more, some of the runners' teammates had even come out of the dugout to get 'in the pickle' with him. Everybody in the stands was laughing so hard, I can't even remember if they tagged him or not. It was something straight out a Keystone Kops' movie."

It was during this time with the Pirates that the most significant change in scouting in Julian's career took place- the Rule 4 Draft in 1965. Before this, a player was open to sign with any team he chose. Conversely, a team could sign as many players as they wished to sign. "It was every man for himself. Whichever scout got there first with a contract was usually the winner." Julian recalls. "Once the Draft started, you could only sign the players you drafted."

"The main thing the Draft did," he continued, "was limit your opportunities. For example, in 1985, I scouted and could have signed both Will Clark and Rafael Palmeiro, who played at Mississippi State and later had excellent major league careers, if it had been the old days. But we (the Reds') were limited to our one first round choice and the club had decided on Barry Larkin, a local Cincinnati boy. We knew neither Clark or Palmeiro would make it to the second round so, we lost our chance with them. Of course, Larkin (an eventual Hall of Fame inductee in 2012) turned out to be a pretty good choice."

Julian's reputation as a quality scout was already well-established because the Pirates chose a young man from Birmingham, Alabama, a player he had personally recommended, with their first choice in that very first Rule 4 Draft. Baseball's drafting system differs dramatically from the other major sports' leagues and it puts a very high stress level on scouts because teams cannot afford to make many mistakes with their high round selections. "A scout that sends in recommendations of players that don't pan out, doesn't stay around long." This was, obviously, not the case with Julian Mock.

Other teams around the league began taking notice of "The Little Professor", a nickname of respect he soon picked up based on his past educational experience as well as his baseball expertise. In 1968, the Cincinnati Reds came calling and Julian listened.

The Scouting Director for the Reds at the time was Rex Bowen who reported to Bob Howsam, the General Manager. One of the first hires Bowen made when he joined the Reds in 1968 was Julian. Bowen had previously served as the Pirates Scouting Director where he had come to know and respect Julian's baseball knowledge when they worked together there. Julian even toyed with the idea of becoming a full-time scout, but Terry and Alan were just 13 and 10, respectively, and he needed to be closer to home so, he took the North Clayton job instead.

Those early years of Julian's tenure with the Reds saw some of the greatest teams in the history of baseball. From 1970 to 1976, Cincinnati's Big Red Machine dominated baseball. During that span the Reds won five division titles, four National League titles, and two World Series (1975 and 1976). Those teams, led by Manager Sparky Anderson, were blessed with great players like Johnny Bench, Tony Perez, Joe Morgan, George Foster, Ken Griffey, Sr., Don Gullett, Pedro Borbon, and Pete Rose. Some are in the Hall of Fame-one, is not.

Julian has some strong opinions on this subject. "Pete Rose was one of the most exciting players I've ever seen. I was there (with the Reds) during the 70's and he lived up to his nickname 'Charley Hustle' every day. It was not a gimmick or hot dog thing he did. He truly played the game the way it is supposed to be played. But I cannot justify him being in the Hall of Fame, in spite of his records, because he just refuses to admit that he gambled on games. I don't put him in the same category as these guys of the steroid and PED era. Those guys cheated on the game of baseball. Their records are tainted and none of them should ever be in the Hall, although I think, one day, some of them might make it. If Pete would just admit that he gambled, opinions might soften on him, but until he does that, I don't think he should be in the Hall."

During those years, Julian continued to contribute to the organization by supplying the club with young players who would bolster the minor league clubs and some who would eventually make it to the big league club. But even if one of his players was not selected, other scouts would ask his opinion on players they were scouting. It was a general rule of thumb around the organization that if Julian liked 'em, sign 'em. If he didn't, get as far away as fast as possible.

One of his many success stories during those years was a young man from Albany, Georgia named Ray Knight. Julian recommended Knight and he was signed in 1972. Knight played a few years in the minors before making the major league club in 1977, replacing Pete Rose at third base. Knight would go on to have a solid career being noted for one major highlight. While playing for the New York Mets, Knight was on second base and would score the eventual winning run against the Boston Red Sox on the famous Bill Buckner error in the 1989 World Series. Knight's second accomplishment is being married to professional golfer, Nancy Lopez.

During these years as a part-time scout during the summers, Julian primarily travelled around Georgia. Many days were spent in the hot, Georgia sun. At the end of the day, however, it was time to eat.

Several fellow scouts who worked with Julian during these years remember him in two ways associated with food. Wilma Mann, his longtime assistant once he was promoted to Scouting Director remembers, "Julian had a running buddy by the name of Joe Mason. They travelled together a good bit during those years and both of them had an affinity for Shoney's. They loved the 'half pound of ground round' special that was on their menu. They'd go out of their way to find a Shoney's even though there were plenty other restaurants they could have chosen. Those two were characters, let me tell you."

Later, however, Julian picked up the nickname "Catfish." One scout told me that every time Julian would sign a player and later, as Scouting Director, when they would sign a highly-sought player, Julian would treat himself to a catfish dinner.

Bo Trumbo, a scout for the Reds in the 90's under Julian, said that the best advice Julian ever gave him was how to find the best place to eat when you were in a small town. He told me, "Find the place where all the pickups are. That's where the locals eat. If you see a bunch of Buick's, keep looking, but if you see those pickups- pull in. It was good advice. I rarely went wrong following that practice."

As hard and as tedious as the scouting routine was during those years, Julian loved it and there was always an itch to expand his involvement. In 1980, he would scratch that itch.

He was approached by Joe Bowen, brother of Rex, now Scouting Director of the Reds, to take on a more active role. He had been Principal at North Clayton for fourteen years and was at the point where he felt like he had accomplished most everything he had set out to do in education. Maybe it was time to do what he had always wanted to do- work in a major league baseball capacity on a full-time basis. Julian and Dot talked it over, prayed about it earnestly, and, finally, made the decision to take the offer being made.

Julian was given the title of Area Supervisor. His territory would cover Alabama, Mississippi, and Louisiana. For the first year, Julian travelled this territory while Dot and ten year-old Christy stayed home in College

Park. But the wear and tear plus the loneliness of being on the road, mainly by himself, took its toll. He decided he would need to move the family to a more centralized part of his territory in order to limit the travel time as well as his time away from home. He and Dot scouted out several locations, finally settling on the town of Daphne, Alabama, a small town in South Alabama near Mobile.

Once they settled into their new home, Dot realized that she needed to have something to take up her time that would also help her stay fit during the day when Christy was in school. That was the beginning of Dot, the avid golfer.

She took some lessons at the local course and began playing on a regular basis. "If the sun was shining and even some days when it wasn't, you could find me on the golf course." she said. "I absolutely loved the game and by playing as much as I did, well, I guess I got pretty good at it. Over the years I've won several club tournaments and I'd still be playing today if I could."

As Area Supervisor, Mock was responsible for sending in reports to the home office on players that had either been assigned to him to scout or those that caught his eye while scouting another player. A player fitting this description turned out to be one of Julian's highest draft picks in 1988.

While attending a game at the University of West Alabama in Livingston, Alabama, the team's second baseman, Jeff Branson, caught his eye. He was intrigued enough by the play of Branson that he decided to stay overnight and catch the team's game the next day. Again, he liked what he saw and after doing some investigative work on the character of the young man and talking to him personally, he decided to file a report. Others from the Reds came down to see him play in later games and all were impressed enough because of Julian's initial keen eye that they made him their first selection in the second round of the 1988 Rule 4 Draft. Branson became a dependable utility infielder for, not only the Reds, but the Cleveland Indians and the Los Angeles Dodgers.

But scouting success is not only measured by the number of years a player they signed plays in the major leagues, but the impact a scout, particularly a caring scout like Julian Mock, can make in the life of a young man. Just ask Chris Hammonds, Mo Sanford, and Rudy Abbott.

Chris Hammonds had a fine career in the major leagues- a career that enabled him to earn enough to have a comfortable lifestyle. But as he will be the first to say, it would not have been possible without the firm direction of Julian Mock. Chris will relate much of his personal story in his testimonial found later in the book but, in essence, he had no direction and was headed for obscurity until Julian pointed him down the right path. "For once in my life I listened to someone and it made all the difference." Hammonds said.

Chris now lives in Oxford, Alabama with his wife, Lynne, and his two sons and daughter. He and Lynne began the Chris Hammonds Youth Foundation, a Christian-based charity, a few years back. If you want to find out more information on this wonderful organization, go to hammondyouthfoundation.com.

You have probably never heard the name, Mo Sanford. He had a short career appearing in about twenty games over a four year span as a right handed pitcher with the Reds, Rockies, and Twins.

Sanford was born in Americus, Georgia but he went to high school in Starkville, Mississippi where he was a phenom. After graduation, the Yankees offered him a $100,000 signing bonus but his mother wanted him to go to college, thinking he could improve his chances of an even bigger and better contract.

Sanford went to the University of Alabama but struggled and never regained his high school dominance. Julian Mock, however, saw something in the boy that others did not. He took a chance and signed him for far less than the Yankees offer but better than anyone else was willing to give, which was nothing. And even though he did not have a stellar major league career, he got his chance. And all because of Julian Mock.

Rudy Abbott grew up in Anniston, Alabama and began earning a reputation as an excellent baseball prospect during his high school years.

Julian scouted him on several occasions and liked what he saw well enough to offer him a contract. That story is one of the most humorous that Julian tells.

"Rudy's father owned a general merchandise store and most of his time was spent behind the butcher counter. We had decided to offer Rudy a $3,000 bonus. I met with Rudy and his dad in the store one day and presented our offer. I looked at his dad who had a very concerned look on his face and asked him if there was a problem. I was concerned that he had thought I had low-balled the offer and he was going to ask for more money and I knew I was offering my max. The man looked at Rudy and said, 'Son, I really want you to play baseball, but there is no way we can afford $3,000.' When I explained that he didn't have to pay, we were giving it to them, he couldn't sign that contract quickly enough."

Rudy Abbott never fully materialized as a player, but he was ultra-successful as a coach. He started his working career as a writer for a newspaper where he caught the attention of officials at Jacksonville State located in Jacksonville, Alabama. He began his career there as the Public Relations and Sports Information Director. Because of his baseball background, he was asked to take over as coach of the team in 1970. Thus began a thirty-one year tenure as the Gamecocks head coach.

Abbott coached Jacksonville State to NCAA Division II national championships in 1990 and 1991. Seven of his teams advanced to the Division II World Series. In 1979, his team started the season with a 29-0 record, an NCAA record for the best start in history. He was named Division II Coach of the Year in 1990. His all time record is 1003-467 (.682) which places him in the top ten list of wins for Division II coaches.

Abbott and Julian have remained life-long friends and the reason is, in Abbott's words, "because Julian Mock cares as much about the person as he does the ballplayer. He stayed in touch with me during my playing days, but he kept in touch afterwards as well. We ran many, many baseball clinics together during my coaching years and he sent me many good players that he had scouted in high school that helped us win a lot of games. Most scouts sign you and forget you. Not Julian."

After nine years of serving as an Area Supervisor, the Reds promoted him to the position of Eastern Cross-Checker. All the Area Supervisor's in the Eastern Region of the US would turn in their recommendations to Julian. He would then review their reports and make his own evaluations which, most of the time, meant personally seeing the player in action. Again, much of his time was spent on the road.

Then, in January of 1991, his big break came. Julian was asked to take over as Scouting Director, a position he held until 1997. While holding this lofty job in the Reds organization, Julian came into close contact with one of the most interesting and quirky individuals ever associated with the game of baseball- owner Marge Schott, the person responsible for his hiring.

Schott was the managing general partner, president and CEO of the Reds franchise from 1984-1999. She was the third woman in baseball history to own a franchise without inheriting it. She is probably best known, however, for her tight-fisted control of expenditures and her controversial behavior during her tenure as owner which included slurs towards African-Americans, Jews, and persons of Japanese ancestry. She was pretty much an all-inclusive bigot. She was banned from running the organization from 1996 to 1998 due to statements she had made in support of German domestic policies of Nazi leader, Adolph Hitler.

Julian recalls having several arguments with her over the years he was Scouting Director, mainly over contract matters. "She was never willing to pay what we felt it would take to sign a player, but most of the time I could convince her. I don't remember ever losing a battle with her."

Schott was known to be stubborn and extremely opinionated in all of her decisions. In 1995, she took offense at the personal lifestyle of the team's manager, Davey Johnson. Johnson was living with his girlfriend without the benefit of marriage. Schott openly told the press in mid-season that Johnson would not return as the Reds manager the following year no matter how well the team did. Even though the Reds won their division, she held true to her word and fired Johnson at season's end.

One reporter called her "The Big Red Headache" in reference to the Big Red Machine.

Julian, now with a need to be closer to a major airport, relocated him and Dorothy again. As Scouting Director, Julian estimated that he spent 70% of his time on the road scouting, 15% in Cincinnati, and 15% at home. In 1993, with Christy now 20 and on her own, they moved to the Peachtree City area, just south of Atlanta's airport, and in 1996 they moved to their current home, also located in Peachtree City.

During all these moves and because of his extensive travel, Julian wanted to make sure one of his most prized possessions never got in the wrong hands. Throughout his scouting years Julian kept a detailed account of every player he had ever scouted. He called this his "Red Book." He once told Dot that if anything terrible should ever happen to him, "Make sure my Red Book goes in the box with me."

One of the key measurements of a team's success as it pertained to scouting and drafting was whether the players drafted made it to the major league or not. Only time could determine if they were a one-year wonder or a ten-year veteran, but to make it at all was a considerable achievement. The reader needs to understand that there are nearly one thousand players selected each year so, the odds are pretty slim that one of your players would make it. The general rule of thumb was that if a draft produced an 8-10% success rate, the team had done well. For the seven years Julian Mock was Scouting Director for the Cincinnati Reds, the team produced an average 14.375% success rate. And of those that made it to the majors, nearly 40% had careers lasting longer than five years.

With all their successes, however, there is always the story of the one that got away. For Julian, it will always be the great New York Yankee shortstop, Derek Jeter.

The year was 1992 and the Reds held the fifth selection that year. The four teams ahead of them made their selections with none taking the young shortstop from Michigan. Julian explains the choice this way:

"There are two factors that come to play when making your selection. The first is the best available player- the kid who had made the biggest and best impression on your scouts. But the second and sometimes more important factor is need. What position does your team need most? We didn't need a shortstop because we already had Barry Larkin. He was a proven All-Star who was on his way to a Hall of Fame career plus we had two other kids in the farm system that were available if we needed them. We needed a power hitting outfielder. Besides, we weren't totally sold on Jeter defensively, so we took a kid out of Florida who could really hit. We passed on Jeter, made our selection, and the Yankees took him with the next pick. Jeter had a great career and our kid was a flop. I've taken a lot of grief over the years for passing on him, but I remind those that bring it up that four other teams passed, too. Go pick on them some!"

So, what are the qualities that make a good scout and, as in Julian's case, a respected Scouting Director? Julian listed seven factors:

(1) First and foremost, you must be able to identify, hire, and train effectively. You can't just use a buddy system and put your favorite people to work for you. There is too much riding on their decisions and if they don't work out, it's your butt on the line as well as theirs.

(2) Make sure the people who work for you can make decisions. There is nothing worse than having someone who is wishy-washy work for you. I wanted my guys to be decisive. If ten other scouts liked a kid but mine didn't, I was willing to work with that as long as he could give me solid reasons for his decision. Also, they must be willing to learn. Unless they were a proven veteran they needed to he ready to listen to my advice.

(3) Communication is key to being an SD. I had as many as 18 Area Supervisors working for me at any given time with each one of them having multiple Recommending Scouts under them. I needed to know where my Area guys were at all times.

(4) You must be organized and you must manage your schedule so that you're not wasting time.
(5) Even though they sometimes can be mundane, your reports must be done in a timely manner. And your scouts had to be honest and trustworthy. A guy who will cheat on his expense report can't be trusted. I was lucky because I had Wilma Mann handling this part of the job for me. She was a tiger when it came to reviewing those expense reports. But even then Marge would often question certain expenses. She'd always come around to my recommendation, but she'd quibble about them nonetheless.
(6) I always wanted to maintain a good reputation among the other organizations and I never wanted my guys to be considered anything less than honorable and trustworthy. My reputation, my good name, is the most important thing I have.
(7) And you had to be a good negotiator. Whether dealing with the prospect, their parents, another ball club, or an agent you must be able to negotiate.

There was one last assignment for Julian. Matters had become tenuous in Cincinnati. Schott's behavior was becoming more and more difficult to deal with. The Commissioner had banned her for three years but, behind the scenes, she still kept a tight rein on financial matters. In 1997, Julian was second in tenure among all of baseball as a Scouting Director, but he was the third lowest paid. At 68, travel was becoming more difficult plus he had been told that he would not be getting a raise, so he decided that maybe now it was time to retire for good. He stepped down as Scouting Director of the Cincinnati Reds in 1997.

But it didn't take long for other teams to get word that he was available and they rapidly contacted him. After consideration and review of his options, Julian agreed to a position with the Arizona Diamondbacks scouting on a professional level. Julian would scout players who were already playing in the Majors- players the D'Backs might want to get in trades, for example.

Finally, two years later, Julian Mock hung up his cleats for good. He settled into his life with Miss Dot in their Peachtree City home and became the doting father and grandfather. Always having a fondness in his heart for his "Murphy boys", he continued to counsel them as they would frequently seek his advice on personal matters.

In the fall of 2013, Julian and Dot were enjoying a quiet evening at home when the phone rang. Julian answered and it was his good friend and scouting protégé, Dan Jennings. Dan (the writer of the Foreward for this book) had worked with Julian for the Reds. He had since become an executive for several major league clubs, most notably the Miami Marlins and now serves as a Special Assistant to the General Manager for the Washington Nationals. Jennings also serves on the Board of Directors for the Professional Baseball Scouts Foundation.

"What's up, Dan?" Julian asked.

"Well, I have some news you might be interested in. I'd like to be the one to inform you that you have been selected as one of 2014's recipients of The Legends of Scouting honor. As you know, since the Baseball Hall of Fame in Cooperstown, New York has never seen fit to include scouts, the lifeblood of baseball, as members this is our own version of the Hall of Fame of Scouts."

The Professional Baseball Scouts Foundation (PBSF) was founded in 2003. PBSF was initially established to financially assist baseball scouts who have fallen on hard times. It is a non-profit organization that relies solely on donations, contributions, and the success of their Annual Awards Dinner/Auction Event where they recognize deserving individuals who have contributed significantly to baseball scouting.

Julian and the family, with the exception of Dot who was dealing with some medical issues, travelled to Los Angeles in January, 2014 where he accepted this most-deserving and incredible recognition.

A man's legacy is made up of many facets, but perhaps, the most significant is how others view him. As can be seen in the Testimonial section that will follow, Julian Mock is a special man. From his days as a young boy playing in the fields of Alabama to his life now as patriarch of his families, both his blood-related and those through association, he will always be held in high regard. Respected, revered, and loved by all, THE MAN IN THE DUGOUT is a giant to those who have had the honor and privilege of knowing him.

7th Inning

"Family Man"

Once upon a time in a land called Alabama in a hamlet called Selma, a young boy grew up with dreams of diamonds. No, not the same kind of diamonds that little girls dream of but diamonds laid out on flat fields made green from the summer sun. Diamonds containing bases spaced exactly 90 feet apart in great arenas where thousands would watch his mighty wooden sword propel the missiles thrown at him over the towering fences out in the field to lead his fellow combatants to victory. This young boy, while not big in stature himself, dreamed of slaying giants. But not just giants- he dreamed of great battles against pirates and tigers and braves.

Not too far from his village was a beautiful, young princess and though they would not meet for many years, the young boy knew he would find her one day. The young lass dreamed of traveling to faraway lands and she, too, knew that one day she would meet and find her one true love. Sir Julian did meet Lady Dorothy one day and they immediately fell in love. They built their castle and were soon blessed with three wonderful children.

Sir Julian realized that his personal dreams of glory and riches on those fields of diamonds were not to be. But that would not stop him from teaching, training, and showing others how to pursue their dreams. So, he set out on his quest. He achieved the highly commendable title of coach. Then, he became the administrator of an educational facility and, finally, he travelled far and wide seeking out those that might have what it takes to make it in what his nation called the Big Leagues. He was awarded many honors for what he accomplished.

Along the way, Sir Julian touched the lives of those he taught, those that toiled with and for him, those that worshipped with him, and those that were fortunate enough to call him family. Sir Julian was a very blessed man, indeed. And because of his dedication, his determination, his faith, and his influence on those he met, he was revered by all who knew him.

One might think by reading the details of the life of Julian Rogers Mock that he did live a fairy tale life. Perhaps he never achieved great wealth. Perhaps he was never acclaimed nationally as a hero. Perhaps he didn't discover a cure for a major disease. In the eyes of some, that would lessen his value as a man. But they would be wrong.

Julian Mock is rich- rich with friends who value his leadership and his willingness to be there for them in good times and bad. He is a hero- just ask those that ever played for him. They call him their mentor, the best coach they ever had, and some even call him a father figure. And somewhere along the way he discovered the formula for bringing out the best in people. But he didn't do it alone. He achieved what he did because of family. And family has always been central in his life.

Let's start with the unsung heroine of this family- Miss Dot. There is a wise saying that says: "Behind every great/successful man there stands a woman." Julian Mock and his three children would say that, in his case, this statement has never been truer. Another saying states that a house is only as strong as its foundation and there is no question that the foundation of the Mock household was and is Miss Dot. This is not said to take anything away from Julian's presence as a father-figure, but to emphasize just how important Dot was to the family. Without someone as strong as Dot, Julian would have never been able to achieve what he did.

When interviewed for Julian's story, his three children (Terry, Alan, and Christy) all requested, in various manners, that the readers of this story understand the significance and importance Dot had in their Dad's success. To do that, let's paraphrase what they told me.

All three stressed the fact that it was their mom who ran the house. Since Julian's work occupied such long hours, Dot was the one who made sure they did their homework, chores, and got to their respective practices on time. And she was also the primary disciplinarian. "We knew better than to get into trouble because Dad made it clear that he expected us to behave correctly," Terry admitted, "but when we did slip up, as kids will always do, Mom was the one who swung the switch."

Alan, too, remembers all the things his mother did for the family. "After we (Terry and Alan) got a bit older, we quit travelling with Dad during the summers when he was scouting. The ongoing maintenance of the household was left up to her. She paid the bills, called the repairmen, everything. And Dad never had to worry about any of that cause he knew Mom was in charge of those matters."

Christy, the youngest, has a little different perspective from Terry and Alan. "Since I came along a little later (she was born 12 years after Alan), I pretty much had Mom to myself after the age of five. Terry and Alan were out of the house in college so I don't think she was quite as strict with me as she had been on them. As a young girl and up through my teenage years, Mom always gave me my privacy. If I was in my room, she would always knock before she came in. I don't know why but I've always remembered that."

Christy also talked about Miss Dot making many of the major purchase decisions without consulting Julian first. "The main big purchase I remember, probably because it affected me directly, is when I turned 16. We went out to a car lot and she bought me a car. You should have seen the look on Dad's face when he got home and saw that car in the driveway. Remember, Dad was very frugal when it came to spending money. But he never said a word. If Momma said it was all right- then it was all right with him." But then she added some very telling words, "I've never considered her the woman behind the man- she's the woman beside the man."

From his days growing up in Alabama to today, spending time with Miss Dot in their beautiful Peachtree City home, family has always been important to Julian. His story would not be complete without listing those in his immediate family who have played such a significant role in making him the man he became and the man he is today.

Peter Robert Mock (father)
Julian's "Daddy" continued working for the Post Office as a rural route carrier for 38 years as well as keeping his hand in farming. Peter remarried and had two girls (half-sisters of Julian who will be listed later) with his second wife. He passed away on November 25, 1975 at the age of 77.

Lanora Rogers Mock (mother)
After her divorce from Peter, she found work at the local hospital, the same hospital where she had given birth to Julian. She never remarried. Sadly, Lanora never fully got over the divorce, carrying resentment and considerable hurt with her the rest of her life. Always the mother, she greeted Julian warmly and affectionately when he would visit, but did not like it when he told her he was going to see his father, who still lived close by. This would create the need for Julian to "sneak around" to visit him without her knowing it; something he never liked doing. Lanora passed away on August 16, 1977 (the same day Elvis Presley died) at the age of 81.

P. R. Mock (brother)
After serving in the United States Navy, P. R. settled in Charlotte, North Carolina. He was a radio operator for Eastern Airlines until they went out of business. At that point, he became an appliance repairman. He had two daughters; Sandy Johnson, a nurse living in Kissimmie, Florida and Libby Petrie, who resides in Charlotte. P. R. had four grandchildren, two by each daughter. He died in 1995 at the age of 69.

James Mock (brother)
Jim and Margaret had been married for 63 years at the time of his death in 2012 at the age of 85. Jim was a real estate broker for most of his career. However, upon his retirement he went to the University of Alabama and

got a degree in business with a minor in accounting. Jim and Margaret then moved to Marietta where they resided until his death.

Jim and his wife had six children, four girls and two boys as well as nine grandchildren.

Linnie Shaw (half-sister)
In a wonderful circle of life story, Linnie, who lives in Selma, Alabama, works as an employee of the US Post Office and maintains the same rural route that Peter, their father, ran for many years. She and her husband, Buck Shaw, have two children.

Earle Jordan (half- sister)
Earle is a graduate of the University of Alabama with a degree in secondary education. She is soon to retire from high school teaching. She and her husband also live in Selma and have two children.

Terry (daughter)
Terry has survived the days of travelling around the south on scouting expeditions and sitting in the dirt to watch her dad coach the Murphy baseball teams. She feels that one of her best attributes is one that was instilled into her by both her mom and her dad- "Mock determination."

She attended North Clayton High School while her father was Principal, but she graduated from Morrow High School. She admits that she had difficulty being the Principal's daughter. Terry holds both a Bachelor of Fine Arts/Drama and a Masters of Psychology degree from the University of Georgia.

Terry has two children; a daughter, Kate and a son, Julian. She is now a fitness trainer living in Decatur, Georgia.

Terry has given permission to include two touching, heartwarming stories involving her dad. The first involves the birth of her daughter. When she presented Julian with his first grandchild he, of course, visited her in the hospital. His present to her was a simple statement of love- one rose in a Coca-Cola bottle. That tradition has been maintained by Terry's daughter who gives her the same gift each year on Mother's Day.

The second event occurred, once again, in a hospital. Terry was due to have surgery and as she awaited the time for the nurses to come get her, the door to her room opened, and it was Julian. "Just want you to know I'll be right here with you." was all he said. "Daddy held my hand as I lay on that gurney all the way down the hall to the operating room." Terry said through tear-filled eyes. "His work ethic, his values, and his character are the things I admire most in him."

Alan (son)
Always a fixture at Murphy games in the early 1960's was a little toddler dressed in a miniature baseball uniform. This toddler was, of course, Alan. You could find him sitting in the dugout talking to the players or acting as the unofficial batboy. The love of baseball was definitely passed on to Alan.

Alan graduated from North Clayton, playing baseball for the aforementioned Bill Kennedy. He thinks that Coach Kennedy modeled much of his coaching style and practices after things he had been taught by Alan's dad. "We lost in the state semi-finals my Junior year and in the finals my senior year and we really didn't have that much talent. I still believe we won a lot of games by the way we took infield. We didn't just practice fielding, we practiced 'taking infield' and I know he got that from Dad because I saw the way he coached Murphy and it was exactly the same."

After high school, Alan married his long-time sweetheart, Joy, in 1978. He attended Auburn, earning a BS degree in Mathmatics and later obtained his Masters in Sports Management Education from Georgia State. Alan followed in Julian's footsteps not only by attending Auburn, but by playing baseball there as well.

He and Joy have a son, Casey, and a daughter, Courtney. Casey lives in Washington, DC and works for Amazon while Courtney lives in

Colorado. Alan and Joy also live in Colorado. Alan is in the retirement industry and serves as a plan administrator/consultant.

Christy (daughter)
Being the third and somewhat later child, Christy shared that her relationship with Dot and Julian was different from her two older siblings. Christy lived in Atlanta until the age of 11 when they moved to Alabama and Julian began scouting full time. She does recall the batting cage that her Dad had built in their back yard.

Christy lives in Alabama with her two children. Caleb is 14 and her daughter, River, is 8. She is a manager of a health food store but says she spends a great deal of her time being a chauffeur for her two children.

Interestingly, all three children cite character as being one of the primary characteristics they saw in their dad. "I'd like to think this was passed on to the three of us. We were blessed to have two wonderful parents. Even though Dad travelled a lot when I was a kid, when he was home, I had his full attention."

All in all, the years have been good for Sir Julian and Lady Dorothy. They have endured some health issues, the loss of loved ones, and maybe a few isolated setbacks, but, for the most part, life has treated them well.

Sir Julian and Lady Dorothy sat by the fire one night in their comfortable home in the land of Peachtree City reflecting on all that had happened to them over the years. They bathed in the glow of the fire but also in the warmth they've come to know through family, friends, and wonderful memories. "You know, Dorothy," Sir Julian said, "I cannot ask for more than what I have had with you, my dear. I would not change a thing." So, Sir Julian and Lady Dorothy lived happily ever after.

Extra Innings

"Testimonials"

Randy Blalock - Author
"During the writing of this story, I spoke to dozens of people who encountered Julian Mock in various phases of his life. During those interviews, not a single person had anything negative to say about him. Some quirky habits, funny anecdotes, to be sure, but nothing bad. What a wonderful legacy that is!"

"If these testimonials seemed slanted towards ex-Murphy students and former players that is because those who played for him had such a high regard for him that they were readily willing to express their feelings for him. There are many more ex-players that I talked with that are not included."

Alan Mock - son
"I am always amazed at how many of Dad's players, both those that played for him and those he scouted, have stayed in touch with him over the years. I think it is attributable to two things: one, Murphy must have been a special place at that time and place in history and two, Dad had a formidable influence on the players he coached and mentored."

"If I had to boil Dad's success as a coach, administrator, scout, and leader down, it would be the word 'character.' He is definitely a man of character and I think that was the most important thing to him to look for as he evaluated players and prospects. He brought out the best in people. And with Mom's support, since she is possibly the strongest person I know, well, that gave him the ability to be who and what he needed to be."

Randy Blalock

Dan Spier, Murphy High School
Dan sums up his feelings for coach Mock with this story: "When I was in 9th grade, coach took a couple of us football players to his alma mater, Auburn, to see a football game. I remember they were playing Chattanooga. We were so thrilled to see all the glitz and glory of a college football game. Of course we took the 'brown bus', Coach's old Chevy station wagon. I remember the worn out seat covers and the smell of old cigars, but the trip was wonderful. Auburn won 30-8 and went on to a 9-0-1 record that year and were named National Champions. My favorite player was Ken Rice, a big All-American tackle who also kicked off-like me. I thought Coach Mock was super nice to do that for us boys. I will never forget it."

Jim Bello – Murphy High School
"Impeccable character, strong leader, teacher, coach, and motivator are just a few of the adjectives I would use to describe Julian Mock. This man means s much to me and all the other young men who played for him at Murphy. He was and still is, a tremendous role model for us all."

Bo Trumbo – Cincinnati Reds scout
Bo Trumbo, a much-respected baseball scout who has worked for several Major League clubs, credits Julian Mock as giving him his first real chance. He made these various comments: "Julian Mock taught me, and for that matter everyone he ever mentored in scouting, how to scout but, more importantly, how to do it ethically and with integrity. If he ever caught you cheating on an expense report, well, that was it for you. Once he had confidence in our abilities, he trusted our judgments completely. If we felt strongly about a player, even though he might not be as sure about his talents, he would let us make the final decision. He also trusted us if the decision went the other way, too. His knowledge about the game of baseball was legendary. But he was a great administrator as well. There was never any question regarding our assignments. Everything was organized to a T. I guess I would use three words to

describe "Catfish"- knowledgeable, trusting, and ethical. A man who has those three qualities is a pretty good man. Julian Mock taught me how to be a good person as well as a good scout."

Harry Lloyd – baseball coach of Westminister High for 37 years
Harry Lloyd, as has been detailed in the text, has had a long-running association with Julian Mock through various clubs and the summer baseball camp they started. He summed up his thoughts very succinctly: "Julian Mock has the best baseball mind I've ever been around."

Nancy Perry Porter – Murphy High School
"I am a 1963 graduate of the great Murphy High School. I say great for many reasons: students, teachers, and wonderful coaches, especially Coach Mock. Our teachers and coaches were mentors of the best quality. They taught us lessons of life; be on time, do your best, respect others, and mind your manners."

"I played several sports there, but my favorite was basketball. Because I was always in the gym, I got to know all the coaches but Coach Mock quickly became one of my favorites. My father was a sports nut, he took me to every game I played, but his favorite sport was baseball. He loved the coaching skills of Coach Mock. Our family became great friends with Coach and his precious wife, Dot. The nights they came to our home were filled with much laughter."

"Coach Mock had a great sense of humor, but he was a disciplinarian who mentored his guys through tough love. He truly cared about his players and taught them more than the sport they were playing. He taught responsibility for your actions and he taught teamwork- the kind of lessons we have all gone on to use in our adult lives."

"I was privileged to get an invitation to his 80th birthday party and the turn out of his former players was great. It was definitely a tribute to a man who was more than a coach. It was to a true Christian mentor who is loved and respected by so many- including me. He is definitely a SPECIAL person."

Carolyn Dowges – counselor, North Clayton High School
"Excellent administrator. Always knew where you stood with him. Julian was feared by some of the teachers but I always felt that was because they had never taken the time to get to know him. Enjoyed working for him."

Randy Carroll – Murphy High School
Randy started out our interview with these words: "He was a guiding force in my life. He was a demanding coach- there is no question about that, but his expectations were the same for everyone on the team. He never showed favoritism to anyone, from his best stars to the kid who just barely made the team and sat on the end of the bench. He was not demonstrative with his instructions. Only one thing got him upset- the lack of hustle. But you know, I don't ever remember any of the guys I played with not hustling. We knew that's what he wanted and we were ready to give it to him."

"I was fortunate to play baseball on the collegiate level at Georgia Tech. Our coach, Jim Luck, scouted Murphy constantly because he knew a Julian Mock-coached player would be ready for college ball. I think that is obvious since so many of us went on to play at Tech."

"The other trait about the Coach that always stood out to me was that he was respectful of all of our opponents and their coaches. He never cut them down in our pep talks or belittled them in any way. No one I ever played for had the baseball expertise of Julian Mock."

George Zuraw – fellow scout with the Cincinnatti Reds
"Julian was a very good baseball man. He rarely used the conventional methods other scouts used (radar guns to clock pitchers, etc.). He used something better- instinct. Enjoyed my time with him."

Chris Hammonds – former MLB pitcher
"I owe my baseball career to Julian Mock. He took a chance on me when others looked the other way. Julian scouted me and talked candidly with me. He didn't try to coddle me- he talked to me straight. I originally went

to UAB, but I didn't last long there for various reasons. Julian had seen me pitch and he told me he was going to monitor my progress, but that he thought I might have what it takes. Later, I enrolled at Gulf Coast Junior College. That, too, didn't work out. Julian came to my house one night to talk about my future with my parents and me. He told me plainly that I was on the brink of blowing my chances and that if I didn't get my head straight he would be through with me. He told me to stay in shape- keep working out and at the end of the season he would come back to check on me. He then looked me square in my eyes and said, 'If you haven't done what I'm telling you to do, I won't even stop the car. I'll keep right on driving.' I had learned my lesson. As promised, he came back to work me out. I guess he liked what he saw because he signed me. I was his 'blue light special'. If not for him, I'm not sure what path my life might have taken."

Floyd Harris – Murphy High School
"I am just like the rest of the guys who were fortunate enough to have played for this incredible man. Coach Mock was extraordinary. He would push you to the extreme and demand perfection and you would go to any length to try and give it to him. He commanded respect from the individual and the team and we loved to respond for him. It is truly amazing to me that I only played for this man for three years and, yet, he has had more impact on my life than anyone else other than my father. I am 68 years old and still have the utmost respect for Coach. I still use the life lessons he imparted to each and every one of those who had the good fortune to have played for him. One last comment- Coach will celebrate his 87th birthday this year. He continues to stay in touch with his boys. God gave him a special gift to coach, instruct, lead, and inspire. He still has it. An amazing man.

Lloyd Harris – Murphy High School
"Other than my Dad, Coach is the most admired and valued friend in my life. In 1961, I moved with my family to Atlanta from Cleveland, Tennessee

and was fortunate to attend Murphy High School as a ninth grader. In Tennessee, I played all sports; B team football, basketball, and my best sport, baseball. When I arrived at Murphy, after home room one day, Coach asked to talk to me about my plans for sports at Murphy. I told him I wanted to play everything. I was then amazed at how much he knew about what I had done, sports-wise, in Tennessee. He even knew who my coaches had been. Coach proceeded to give me a fatherly talk about those plans and he shared with me his thoughts about what I should do. At the time, his advice was disappointing to me. His advice was to concentrate on baseball, play basketball, and forget football. He told me my future, based on what he knew about me, was baseball and playing football would risk injury and adversely affect my future in baseball. I was very disappointed in his advice being the 'jock' I thought I was. I talked to my brother about Coach's advice and ultimately followed it. Over the years, looking back at what he told me, I realized it was one of the best things I ever did. That is the kind of man Coach is. He has always known the best and gave excellent advice with only the individual's interest at heart. I love and deeply respect this man."

John Callahan and Leon Norton – Southwest High School
Both men stressed that even though Julian was not much older than they were when they played for him, he demanded respect and discipline. Callahan called him "hard-nosed" and Norton referred to him as "dedicated to getting the best out of us."

Dan Tate – Murphy High School
"Coach Mock took a group of youngsters, polished their raw skills and taught them how to understand and play baseball. During my years on the team, we did not have a roster full of especially talented players (particularly in the hitting department) so we frequently had to scratch out runs against talented opposition. Coach Mock had a knack for manufacturing an unimaginable number of runs out of a couple of infield singles,

a walk, opportune base running, and an error or two. That's what breaks ball games wide open. By the same token, we would spend hours taking infield, preparing for game situations, and going over baseball strategy. We were rarely confused or panic-stricken in games because we had already practiced what to do whatever the situation."

"Coach Mock taught us how to play hard but within the rules; to hustle all the time, especially after making an error; to give a teammate an encouraging pat on the back after he had struck out, and to hate losing with all of our being, but to shake the opponent's hand and look him in the eye in victory or defeat. He taught us lessons about life that we not have grasped and applied until long after graduation when they would be far more important than a high school baseball game. And he made us feel good about it and made it all fun (for the most part)."

Wayne McDaniel – Murphy High School
Wayne contributed much to this effort by detailing some of the game stories that are mentioned in Coach Mock's story. He added this personal note: "There are so many stories to tell about Coach Mock and the young men he had such a profound effect on that there is no way to mention them all. Just know that there are many, many ways Coach Mock influenced mine and others lives."

Robert Koontz – baseball scout
"Let me sum up my feelings for Julian Mock this way- I consider him my second dad. He hired me while with the Reds and even though I was only with the organization four years, he taught me so much. The thing I remember most about Julian was when you'd bring a prospect to him. You'd think he was spending his own money out of his pocket. You would never tell him what the prospect wanted because he'd always think it was too much. What you'd tell him is 'I think I can get it done for this.' (the figure you felt it would take to sign him) Julian Mock has forgotten more about scouting than most scouts know."

Ronald "Butch" Crook – Murphy High School

"If you went to Murphy, then you know of, or have heard the stories about the legendary baseball coach, Julian Mock, known to most of us as, simply, Coach. He was instrumental in my getting the first full baseball scholarship to Georgia Tech, without which I was headed to the US Army. He was also responsible for my tenure in professional baseball, first with Houston and then with the Cincinnati Reds. But what I remember most about Coach was his sincere love for his students, players, and their parents. I had been out of high school several years and the day after Christmas in 1966, my dad died suddenly from heart failure. My dad and I were very close and I was living his dream of playing pr baseball. The burial was held in Atlanta on Candler Road on a cold and rainy day. As I looked up as the service ended, standing there in the rain was Coach."

"One other memorable moment was when my twin boys, Jay and Josh, were playing baseball for South Gwinnett High School. I had gone by the school to watch practice and when I got there I saw Coach Mock standing there talking to Coach Sawyer from South. I called my sons over to introduce them to Coach Mock and before I could say anything, they said, 'We know who he is- we've heard about him all our lives.' That was and is Coach."

Ken Mozley – Murphy High School

"Back in the 1960's when we were teenagers and each of us were establishing our individuality and direction in life, we were influenced by several different people. Influence obviously came from our parents, but also from peers, teachers, and, for some of us, our coaches. Outside of the time we spent with our parents, our high school coaches had our attention more than anyone else."

"From this perspective, Coach Julian Mock entered the lives of all of us who played baseball under his coaching and guidance. When playing baseball for Coach Mock, you were taught to (1) wear your uniform like a professional (he even demonstrated how to put it on from the socks all the way up to the cap), (2) learn the fundamentals of the game to the level that it became 'part of your being', and (3) play the game and execute these fundamentals with the determination and commitment to being the BEST. What became obvious about Coach from the very first practices was his interest in each player learning their specific position and what was expected. It didn't matter whether you were a pitcher, catch, infielder, or outfielder, there was going to be time in practice where you and your position were given his total attention and instruction. And everybody else had better be listening as well."

"Anyone who played for Coach could tell you his influence continued far beyond their time in high school and on the baseball field. No one would tell you he was easy on them because he wanted each person to reach their highest potential. He developed determination and confidence in his players, some very talented and easy to develop and some not so talented. But he still spent time with each to improve their skills. I never played on one of Murphy's Championship teams, but there was never any doubt that I played for a Championship Coach."

Wilma Mann – Cincinnati Reds

"My position with the Cincinnati Reds spanned thirty-seven years, the last ten as the Director of Scouting Administration. During my tenure, I had thr opportunity of working with numerous General Managers and Scouting Directors and one of those Scouting Directors was Mr. Julian Mock."

"Julian was a very personable and professional individual. He was hard working and dedicated to his profession. He expected great things of himself and in return he expected others to perform in a professional manner. Julian's greatest asset was being a great evaluator of baseball talent. My husband, Millard, who is very fond of Julian, expressed to me in a conversation after returning from a tryout of elite players, 'If the scouts get the players to attend Julian's tryout camps, he can tell them if they can play at a professional level.' Julian was very serious about his position, but he also had a lighter side. He used his sense of humor often."

"An outstanding teacher who received the highest praise from those that were taught by the master, such as Thomas Wilson, Clay Daniel, Bo Trumbo, Robert Koontz, David Jennings, and Tom McDevitt among others. A gentleman with the highest respect and regard for others. After accomplishing an arduous task he often said, 'It is time to have a little fun.'"

"My years of working with Mr. Mock were some of the most enjoyable of my career. It was a pleasure and I will always wish him the very best."

<u>Cleve Fowler – Murphy High School</u>
"Beyond his coaching success at every level of sports to his success as a scout and executive in the major leagues, Julian Mock has been a teacher, friend, and mentor to hundreds, and maybe thousands, of men and women throughout his various careers. Coach Mock has been my coach, friend, and mentor since the fall of 1958. He was my first basketball coach in my first year of high school. I played B team football and varsity baseball for him and, in my opinion, there has never been anyone better to teach young people the fundamentals of sports, sportsmanship, and solid life values. He was a pioneer in making metro-Atlanta a hot bed of baseball talent. After high school, Coach became my friend, Julian; and I knew that he was always willing to help me if needed. I consider it an honor to have played for him and to know him as much more than a coach. Next to my family, there is no one that has had a more positive influence in my life."

Cleve also had this to say about Miss Dot: "I can't say enough about the loving patience, dedication, and understanding displayed by Dot, Julian's wife, over the years. All of us who played for Coach became her second family; her 'boys'. And when we married and started having our own families she embraced our wives with the same kind of love and kindness that she had given us. I'm sure that extra burdens were placed on her due to Coach's travels as a scout, but she handled them with tremendous grace."

Roy Jarrett – Murphy High School

"It was a pleasure and rewarding experience to be a part of what I will call the Murphy baseball team dynasty years from 1960-1963. Coach Mock's War Eagles won four straight City Championships and several State Championships."

"Our coach, Julian Mock, molded some good athletes to become better players than they knew possible. How did he do this? If practice makes perfect, the Eagles practiced long and hard. If the weather was bad, you practiced in the gymnasium. During Spring break, you practiced from 9 am til dusk with a break for lunch. There was the usual batting and fielding sessions but the added dimension was on situations and details of what you needed to do during the game. Then, when game time rolled around you were on auto pilot with no bonehead plays being made. Baseball was serious business for Coach and if you wanted to remain in good standing, it had to be serious to you. Just watching our teams take infield practice had to be demoralizing to our opponents."

"Several of us wondered if Coach could smile but that was undetermined. His dry sense of humor made us laugh but did he smile? By now you may liken Coach to a Drill Sergeant of baseball skills and fundamentals. If you reached that conclusion, you would be correct. His players would storm the gates for him as we loved him for his devotion and commitment to make us better at a game we loved as much as him. This discipline he taught on the diamond rolled over to real life personal habits."

"On the flip side of getting better playing ball was the mental part of it which included the dreaded fine box. Play smart, not dumb included a lengthy list of mental errors like failure to miss a sign, taking a called third strike, missing the cutoff man, not running at full speed, etc. There are certain things you must not do on the field or off of it. The money was used for a team party."

"My personal story relates to my inclusion in this four year dynasty. I had made the decision that I wasn't going to play baseball but as I was walking home from school one day, Coach pulled up in his station wagon and said tersely, 'Jarrett, get in the car!' (no please you notice) "Why weren't you at practice?' I muttered something back to him but it did not resonate. Then, there was a quiet period which seemed like an eternity before he stopped in front of my home and simply said, 'See you at practice tomorrow! No excuses!' You just did not tell Coach no because you respected and admired him. He is one of those rare folks I could never say no to his face."

"After Murphy, I went on to a top academic school (Georgia Tech) on a football scholarship with the stipulation that I could play baseball in the Spring. Joining me at Tech on the baseball team were six other Murphy grads. That meant seven players from the same high school playing Division I baseball on scholarships concurrently. This is probably an NCAA record that has gone unreported anywhere. We all owe our gratitude to Coach for preparing us for this opportunity as he expected you to perform on the field and in the classroom."

"There are a lot of clichés I could conclude with but simply put, he was like a father, minister, role model, teacher, and friend to me. Coach, I will be eternally grateful to you for making me a better baseball player and a better man."

"Love you, Coach."

Acknowledgements

The author wishes to express his sincere thanks to all those who had a part in the writing of this book. To those interviewed either by phone or in person. To those who contributed testimonials. To those who provided ideas. To all of you- thank you.

A big thanks goes out to my good friend, Jerry Owen (Murphy, Class of 1966), for planting the seed for the book. Last August, at our 50th Reunion as I was promoting my book, THE MANY WALKS OF LIFE, Jerry approached me one morning and said, "You should write a book about Coach Mock." You were right!

To Mike and Chance Bentley of Bentley Photography in Winder, Georgia, for their front and back cover design work. They reworked a picture of the Coach that originally appeared in Murphy's 1964 annual, enhancing it and adding the title as well as designing the picture and copy appearing on the back cover. Check out their work at www.bentleyphotography.com.

To my three drivers: Floyd Harris, Lloyd Harris, and Ken Mozley who made sure I made it to Peachtree City for my interviews with Julian while I was not able to drive long distances.

To my "editor" Joann Smith for making sure my commas, semi-colons, and periods were all in the right places.

And, finally, for the support and appreciation I received from all of Coach's "Murphy Boys".

About the Author

Randy Blalock has been married to Cindy for 28 wonderful years. They live in Winder, Georgia and are both active members of Winder First United Methodist Church where Randy teaches an adult Sunday School Class and leads the 11:00 pm Christmas Eve Candle Lighting Service each year as lay pastor.

Randy spent his working career in the banking industry and now spends his retirement time writing, reading and watching too much TV. He is inching ever closer to his goal of visiting every major league baseball stadium and should satisfy that goal in 2017- as long as they don't build any new stadiums. On football Saturdays in the fall, you can find him in Sanford Stadium cheering for the Georgia Bulldogs.

Randy has two children and two grandsons; two "adopted" grandchildren; and a great-niece, Ella Mae Akins, that he has fallen in love with. His hobbies are reading, playing trivia games (don't call him when *Jeopardy! i*s on), and watching sports either in person or on TV.

Randy is the author of three children's books: *Which Cloud Does God Live In?*, *The Magic Ornament*, and *Randolph: The Forgotten Reindeer*. He has also written the fictional novel *THE MANY WALKS OF LIFE*. His novel is available at Amazon.com. If you are interested in learning more about his work or would like to order one of his previous books, please check out his website at www.randyblalockauthor.com. Also, check out his author page on Facebook and Pinterest.

Made in the USA
Lexington, KY
24 June 2016